D1524314

EXETER HISPANIC TEXTS

Founded by Keith Whinnom and J. M. Alberich

General Editor: W. F. Hunter

LII

BOOK OF DEVOTIONS

—

LIBRO DE DEVOCIONES Y OFICIOS

EXETER HISPANIC TEXTS

General Editor: W. F. Hunter

Volumes prior to Volume XXXI are available while stocks exist from the Department of Spanish, University of Exeter.

Constanza de Castilla

BOOK OF DEVOTIONS
—
LIBRO DE DEVOCIONES Y OFICIOS

Edited by
Constance L. Wilkins
Miami University

UNIVERSITY
of
EXETER
PRESS

First published in 1998
by University of Exeter Press
Reed Hall, Streatham Drive
Exeter, Devon EX4 4QR
UK

ISSN 0305–8700
ISBN 0 85989 487 8

British Library Cataloguing in Publication Data
A catalogue record for this book
is available from the British Library

Printed and bound in Great Britain by
Short Run Press Ltd, Exeter

ACKNOWLEDGMENTS

This edition of Sor Constanza's devotionary is the result of a longstanding desire to make available more texts written by medieval Hispanic women authors. The work on this edition has led me in many unexpected directions and has been enriching in surprising ways. In some ways I shall miss this daily contact with my fifteenth-century namesake. I owe a debt of gratitude to a number of people and institutions. First, I should like to acknowledge the assistance of Miami University, Oxford, Ohio, in the form of grants and research leaves in 1991 and 1996. The Department of Spanish and Portuguese has also supported my work on the project in numerous ways. Furthermore, a major grant from the National Endowment for the Humanities in 1995-1996 made continued work on the edition possible. I wish to express my special appreciation to Dr. William Hunter, General Editor of Exeter Hispanic Texts, for his meticulous examination of the entire text and for his valuable suggestions which have resulted in the production of a much more accurate and comprehensive edition. I must also thank Betty Marak for the attractive appearance and accuracy of the final typescript. Her skill and perseverance saw me through nearly a dozen versions of the text. It would not be possible to mention all those who in some way assisted me or influenced my work on the book. Since I did not accept all the suggestions offered to me, I must claim responsibility for all errors and failings in the edition. Nonetheless, I should like to acknowledge the assistance of Dr. Stephen Nimis in clarifying several problems in the Latin text; the help of the staff of the Sala Cervantes in the Biblioteca Nacional in Madrid; the thoughtful counsel and enthusiastic interest of Fr. Ramón Hernández, O.P., General Archivist of the Dominican Order at Santa Sabina Church in Rome and of Sister Carmen González, O.P., Archivist of the Real Monasterio de Santo Domingo in Caleruega; and the prayerful support of the many Dominican sisters in Spain, Italy, and the United States with whom I have discussed the prayer book. Finally, and yet most importantly, my heartfelt gratitude goes to two people whose contributions and dedication made this book possible: to Dr. Heanon Wilkins for his steadfast support, encouragement, and help from the very beginning, and to Fr. Gabriel O'Donnell, O.P., for the insights, good cheer, inspiration, and wisdom that helped lead me to a deeper understanding of Constanza's prayer book.

INTRODUCTION

The Author

Constanza de Castilla was the prioress of the monastery of Santo Domingo el Real in Madrid from approximately 1416 to 1465, relinquishing the position only a few years before her death in 1478. Although we know that she was, in fact, a princess, the granddaughter of King Pedro I, little is known about her life before becoming prioress. Constanza's father, Juan de Castilla, was the son of a questionably legal marriage between Pedro I and a noblewoman, usually identified as Juana de Castro. After the murder of King Pedro, his son Juan was viewed as a potential threat to the Trastamara dynasty and was imprisoned for most of his adult life in northern Castile, where he married his jailer's daughter, Elvira de Falces. It is likely that Constanza and her brother also spent much of their youth in prison apartments. Various histories indicate that Constanza entered the convent at a young age, having been rescued from imprisonment by Queen Catalina, wife of Enrique III and Constanza's cousin.[1] Even though the dynastic dispute had been resolved by the early fifteenth century, surely Constanza's familial relationship to the royal house carried with it both advantages and disadvantages. Still, during her long tenure as prioress, the convent reached its greatest prominence and prosperity,

---

[1] For information on Juan de Castilla and on Constanza's early life and entry into the convent, see Sitges 447-52 and *Historia del Rey* 259.

receiving special protection and favor from monarchs who seemed pleased to acknowledge Constanza as cousin or aunt.

Archival documents and Church historians refer to Constanza as an honest and devout religious woman. It is likely that she entered the convent first in Toledo, but the earliest documents from Santo Domingo el Real in which Constanza's name appears already refer to her as prioress. Although we do not know the year of her birth, she must have been only in her twenties when she assumed leadership of the community. Documents from 1419 to 1422 enumerate extraordinary privileges granted to Constanza by the provincial prior.[2] Some documents deal with exemptions from the usual restrictions and obligations observed by all cloistered nuns, while a number of other provisions sought by Constanza were designed to maintain her own power, to sustain that of future prioresses, and to safeguard the material well-being of the community. She was responsible not only for expanding and restoring her own convent but also for founding another in Toledo. Constanza had extensive responsibilities, possessions, authority, and autonomy. She had absolute fiscal control over convent estates and possessed personal property and real estate, with the right to control it as she saw fit. It is apparent that Constanza was a woman of influence and power both within and outside of her convent.

Evidently Sor Constanza did not maintain the kind of separation from the outside world that one might expect inasmuch as all nuns had been strictly cloistered since the decree by Pope Boniface VIII at the end of the thirteenth century. The prioress and her convent were surely affected by social, political, and ecclesiastical changes occurring around them. The impact on the nuns of local and national events is seen in a document (Archivo Histórico, carpeta 1365, no. 7), which describes the negotiations between Constanza and the men of the city council regarding the town's

---

[2] Archivo Histórico Nacional, Madrid, Clero, Carpeta 1365, nos. 5 and 9. Examples of the special privileges granted to Constanza are: permission to have her servants or female relatives eat with her and sleep in her room, permission to speak to her relatives or others without wearing her veil, and permission to have a private walled garden with a door leading to it from her quarters.

contribution to the convent. The economic demands of the wars the king was involved in made it difficult for the town to maintain the former level of material support for the convent. It was a period of growth of the city of Madrid, already an important urban center and the habitual residence of the monarchs who ruled during Constanza's lifetime. Constanza had permission to conduct convent business at the royal palace, located near Santo Domingo el Real. In the ecclesiastical realm, the Dominican Order in Spain was undergoing a process of extensive reform in the fourteenth century. It may be that the concern Constanza expresses for the education of the nuns under her care reflects one of the new stipulations of the Order that all correction and penance of female religious must be the responsibility of the prioresses. As Penelope D. Johnson points out in her book *Equal in Monastic Profession*: "The world of the medieval nun was not isolated from its surrounding lay community; rather, it was connected by family, regional, and ecclesiastical ties" (100).

Ties to family were supposed to be severed when one entered a monastery; however, many nuns did not give up these links to their birth family, rather they added a second family of the convent. Like Constanza de Castilla, many medieval women who entered the convent were well-born and maintained their sense of social position and confidence. References to Constanza's royal lineage appear prominently in convent documents, and her tomb in the Archeological Museum in Madrid also emphasizes her nobility in the inscription above the sepulcher and in the prominent coat of arms of Castile at the base of the tomb. After many years of effort, the prioress succeeded in gaining royal permission to build a chapel at Santo Domingo el Real in which to reinter the remains of her father and grandfather.[3] Constanza's connection with her family is also evident in her prayers for the souls of her deceased relatives and for the well-being of the king (fol. 26r). Her requests that the king be freed from treason and threats and that his crown be exalted indicate her awareness of and concern for current political problems (fol. 27r). There is no evidence in the devotionary that Constanza saw her royal connection as

---

[3] For provisions regarding the chapel and the authority granted to Constanza by Enrique IV, see Archivo Nacional, carpeta 1365, no. 21.

a spiritual problem. Her continuing family contacts and her activities outside the convent were undoubtedly advantageous to the material prosperity of the community. Bonnie S. Anderson and Judith P. Zinsser in *A History of Their Own* stress that because of her activities outside the convent, the prioress was likely to be the one most affected by the lack of isolation from the outside world and most in jeopardy regarding her holy vows (203). Constanza was, however, aware of the threat that her outside activities posed to her spiritual well-being. She expresses her concern with the problem of separation from the temptations and values of the world as she prays to be taken away from "las conversaciones dañosas a mi ánima, e de los negocios del mundo en que me yo ocupo" (fol. 5r).

The Work

Scholarship on medieval and early modern women has become increasingly abundant in the past two decades, and great strides have been made, through study of archival documents, in understanding the social, legal, and economic situation of medieval Iberian women. Nonetheless, the near invisibility of women as subjects in medieval Spain continues to be a matter of concern and frustration to scholars. The prayer book written by Constanza de Castilla is an important part of the small body of writing by medieval Spanish women available to us today, providing us with not only another woman's voice but also a different sort of writing from the memoirs of Leonor López de Cordoba, the spiritual treatises of Teresa de Cartagena, and the poetry of Mayor Arias and Florencia Pinar.

Sor Constanza's devotionary, written principally for private use within the walls of her convent, is meant to aid in the spiritual perfection of the writer and of the nuns in her community. The limited use for which the book was intended and the author's relationship with the royal family may have protected her from the anxiety of the Church and society about female erudition and spirituality. In fact, no mention was made of Constanza's writing in the Church histories of the seventeenth century that praise her work in the Madrid convent nor in the early twentieth-century history of the community by the noted Dominican Luis G. Alonso Getino. The devotionary has received critical attention only in the last few years. An article by Ana María Huélamo de San José in 1992 described the manuscript, commented on its contents, and identified its author. In 1995, Ronald E. Surtz dedicated a chapter of his book *Writing Women in Late Medieval and Early Modern Spain* to Constanza and her prayer book, and Ángela Muñoz Fernández also included a chapter in her book *Acciones e intenciones de mujeres en la vida religiosa de los siglos XV y XVI*.

Sor Constanza's book of prayers and devotions exists in a single manuscript, MS 7495 of the Biblioteca Nacional in Madrid, which has never been edited previously. Little is known about the history of the codex, but it is likely that it remained in the convent of Santo Domingo el Real of Madrid until the demolition of the original convent buildings in the nineteenth century, around 1868, at which time it probably entered the National Library's collections. Although many medieval Spanish manuscripts are known or presumed to be copies of lost originals, in this case there are a number of features that could support the theory that the extant manuscript is a scribal copy made at the behest of the author (see below, p. xvi). The fifteenth-century Gothic script, contemporary with the lifetime of the author, and the richness of the codex, written on parchment with illustrated capitals and several decorated pages, lend weight to this hypothesis. The nature of the text is also particularly significant in this regard. Like many other works by women writing during the late medieval and early modern periods, Constanza's prayer book was not intended for publication or wide distribution, but rather for personal use by the author and for communal worship among the nuns in her convent.

The devotionary, written half in Latin and half in Spanish, begins with a prayer that comprises almost the first third of the book. This prayer, intended for private devotions, focuses on the life and passion of Christ and the succeeding events, ending with Pentecost. It is followed by three liturgical offices in Latin, including the Hours of the Nails, which is given in both languages. While celebrations of the Holy Cross and the instruments of the Passion, including the lance and the nails, were well known in the fifteenth century, there is no evidence of other celebrations dedicated solely to the nails. In his history of the Dominican Order, Juan López indicates that the Office written by Sor Constanza was celebrated with special papal permission (10).

The book contains the following sections:

Prayer on the life and passion of Christ, supplications, post-Passion events, and Pentecost. The prayer is divided into 44 chapters of unequal length, but similar format. After the climactic moment of the death of Jesus in chapter 34, the author incorporates elements of the Divine Office, for example, the Kyrie, Good Friday Improperia, the Creed, the Song of the Three Young Men from the book of Daniel, adoration of the Cross, three hymns, and various prayers (fols. 1-31v)

Office for Advent, including the complete cycle of Canonical Hours (fols. 31v-41v)

Mass of the Incarnation of Christ (Christmas Mass) (fols. 41v-44r)

Office in commemoration of the nails of the passion of Christ, comprising an entire sequence of Canonical Hours with the Mass between Prime and Terce (Latin fols. 44r-58v, Spanish fols. 58v-74v), supplication to Christ and prayer to the guardian angel (fols. 74v-75r)

Fifteen joys of the Virgin, with a supplication and a protestation (fols. 75r-78v)

Seven sorrows of the Virgin, with a supplication (fols. 78v-79v), followed by a Marian litany (fols. 79v-82v)

Prayer to Christ including a listing of the contents of the work, a supplication, and a protestation (fols. 82v-83r)

Prayer of praise and adoration of Jesus (O bone Jesu) (fols. 83v-84r)

Athanasian Creed (fols. 84r-86r), Psalm 21 (fols. 86r-87v), Pentecost liturgy (fols. 87v-88r)

Magnificat with liturgical responses (fols. 88r-89r), Psalm 88 (fols. 89r-91r)

Affirmations of faith and prayers for salvation, contemplation of the Host, supplication (fols. 91v-93r)

Prayer for whose recitation the Pope grants 2000 years of pardon (fol. 93v)

Letters between St. Ignatius, the Virgin, and St. John in Spanish and in Latin (fols. 94r-97r)

Questions to ask persons on the verge of death (fols. 97r-99r)

Saint's prayer (fols. 99r-100v)

Author's supplication on the day of her death (fols. 101r-102v), litany (fol. 103r)

Reference to and quotations of scriptural passages occur frequently in the devotionary. The author especially cites the psalms in the liturgical sections of her book and the synoptic gospels in her prayer on the life and passion of Christ. Owing to the importance of study and contemplation in Constanza's life and the devotional character of her book, the text also contains many quotations and scattered words and phrases from other biblical, liturgical, and devotional texts. Although all these religious sources are such as one would expect an educated nun to be exposed to, it is fascinating to imagine just how integral a part of her normal thought processes these phrases and words had become. Like most monastics, she would have had all these elements in her mind without any particular awareness of a distinction between them. Moving from one source to another or even one language to another was a very natural transition for her. In the liturgical offices in Latin a given passage of a half dozen lines might incorporate three or four fragments from different scriptural sources (see below, p. xxi).

A primary importance of the book lies in what it reveals about the spiritual life of this self-proclaimed *esclava de Dios* and of her convent sisters. Throughout the prayer book we see the interaction between the personal and the more didactic or doctrinal aspects of Constanza's desire to praise and serve God and to aid in the spiritual perfection of herself, her sisters in the convent, and others who may use her book.[4] Historical documents indicate more about secular and material aspects of Constanza's life, while the prayer book provides evidence of her spirituality and her attitudes toward the sacred and its reflection in her life. Constanza's devotionary reveals a liturgically organized life. For much of the

---

[4] For example, contrast the objective, theological affirmation: "En ese momento el tu santíssimo spíritu fue apartado del tu santísimo cuerpo. Yo creo verdaderamente que la tu divinidat sienpre estudo contigo en la cruz e en el sepulcro e decendió a los infiernos con el spíritu" (fols. 18v-19r) with the great emotive force of her detailed admission of sinfulness in the supplication on fols. 20r-22r.

medieval world, but especially for religious women who consecrated their lives to the service of God in prayer, the liturgical seasons of the year reflected the important events in the life of Christ, and the canonical hours marked the rhythm of each day.[5] Nearly every day of their lives Constanza and other cloistered nuns performed certain activities, said certain prayers, and sang certain hymns. The organization of their time as well as their predominant values and preoccupations, such as concern with pride, obedience to the commandments and to the rules of the Order, diligence in participating in the Divine Office and in fulfilling their vows, are specific to that way of life. The prayer book reflects behaviors and attitudes that are the result of personal and spiritual development in response to the monastic life surrounding Constanza. This prayer book, written by a woman to be used primarily by herself and by other women, provides moving evidence of the beliefs, experience, and expression of a religious woman in Spain of the later Middle Ages.

The Manuscript

Title and Authorship

Various titles have been used to refer to MS 7495, *olim* X.307 and 104.4. The card catalogue in the Sala Cervantes lists the codex as *Libro de*

---

[5] The liturgy of the Mass and the Divine Office used by Sor Constanza and proper to the Dominican Order was adopted from the rite in use in the Roman basilicas in the thirteenth century. The Franciscans adopted and popularized the rite of the Roman curia, a shorter and somewhat simplified form of celebration. In the mid-sixteenth century, the latter became the Roman rite, to be used by all orders and dioceses without a proper rite in continual use for more than a hundred years. The Dominican rite, not seriously altered until the reform of the liturgical psalter in 1930, was very influential in the liturgical observances of other orders. It is characterized by its simplicity and austerity, the excellence of its hymns and responsories, and its doctrinally nuanced selection of scriptural and patristic texts. For additional information on the Dominican rite, see Bonniwell. For a brief summary, see Sheppard 90-94. The liturgical seasons (Advent, Christmas, Septuagesima, Lent, Easter, and the time between Pentecost and Advent) and the canonical hours (Matins, Lauds, Prime, Terce, Sext, None, Vespers, and Compline) are the same for Dominicans and all other Roman rites.

oraciones compuestas y ordenadas por una monja dominica, and the catalogue of liturgical manuscripts in the National Library and the *Inventario general* call it *Libro de horas y devocionario.*[6] The spine of the modern binding reads *Devocio y oficio* in gold letters on a dark red background. The manuscript itself, however, contains neither a title page nor a title on the first page above the opening prayer.

The first lines of the text identify the author by her vocation as a sister in the Order of Saint Dominic. Further third-person references to "la dicha soror," author and compiler of the prayers and offices, occur at the beginning of several major sections of the book (folios 31v, 44r, 75v, and 78v). The author identifies herself as Costança or Constança six times within the prayers. There is, however, no real evidence that this is an autograph manuscript, but neither can the possibility be totally discarded. It is more probable that Constanza followed the usual custom of dictating the prayers and offices to scribes. The regularity and calligraphic nature of the letters in all the hands are characteristic of writing produced by professional scribes.

Description and Condition

The manuscript consists of 103 parchment folios divided into thirteen quires with catchwords at the end of every eighth folio. The folios measure 165 x 115 mm with a text block of 122 x 82 mm ruled in blue ink. Most pages contain twenty-two lines of script in a single column extending across the text block. Of the twenty-four pages that contain only twenty-one lines, eight have ruling for twenty-two lines with the last line left blank. Folios 101 and 102 have only eighteen lines of script with the text block measuring 115 x 76 mm. There is no ruled text block on folio 103r, and cursive writing of the fifteenth century fills the entire page. Five pages have additional lines of text below the text block: 14r, 44v, 45r, 78v, and 79r. Folios 44v and 45r have frame-ruling to contain the added lines that are to be inserted earlier on the page.

---

[6] For other descriptions of MS 7495 see: Domínguez Bordona I, 277; Huélamo San José 134-35; Janini and Serrano 93-95; *Inventario general de manuscritos* XII, 109.

The manuscript is written in a very regular Gothic script of the fifteenth century. A change in scribal hand is evident on folios 99r-100v, 101r-102v, and 103r, thus indicating a total of at least four different hands. Corrections, brief interlinear insertions, and marginal notes that contain words to be added to the text occur with greatest frequency in the first thirty-one folios. The corrections and added lines are contemporaneous with the style of the body of the text. There are usually not enough differences in the script of the marginal notes and corrections to indicate a different hand from the main text.[7]

The portions of the book in Latin and the devotions derived from other sources have fewer marginal notes. The infrequent corrections that do occur in these sections tend to be minor orthographic changes, such as the addition of an initial *h* or a second *r* in a word like *error*. In contrast, the majority of substantive corrections and additions occur in the most original and most personal parts of the book, that is, the life and passion of Jesus on folios 1r-31v and the prayer to the Virgin on folio 78r-v. This may indicate that special attention was paid to those sections, possibly by the author herself. However, it is also logical that correctors would feel more free to change the original portions than the liturgical offices or the sections that are adaptations of other sources.

In *Manuscritos con pinturas*, Jesús Domínguez Bordona notes the deteriorated condition of the manuscript. The first several folios have suffered the most damage, with torn edges, diagonal creases across the pages, and brown spots, especially at the top of the folios. Many letters toward the bottom of the pages are barely legible. Nearly a sixth of the pages are difficult to read owing to faded letters and background shadow. There are some spots, smudges, and small holes randomly throughout the codex, but they do not generally impair legibility. Occasional blank spaces may have contained a letter that was erased or has faded away.

---

[7] I should like to thank Sr. Lorenzo Martín del Burgo, librarian in the manuscript section of the Biblioteca Nacional, for consulting with me and for sharing his paleographic expertise regarding questions of dating and identification of scribal hands.

Decoration of the Text

Rubrics, chapter headings, and other internal divisions like *oración*, *verso*, *responso*, etc., are written in red in contrast to the black ink used for the rest of the text. Blue paragraph signs occur sparingly in the longer lessons on folios 49 to 51 and 61 to 67, while alternating red and blue ones are abundant in the prayer on folios 101r to 102r. Red is also used in designs that cover changes or corrections, fill the space at the end of a line, or at times indicate that a completion to the line was to be recited or sung. These designs are in the form of either an abstract swirl for the space of a letter or two, or a decorative rectangle that may at times extend for two or three lines.

Decorative capital letters, two lines high at the beginning of sections or one line high within the prayers, are red and blue with alternation of the predominant color. There are no historiated capitals. Fine floral, vine-like designs extend into the margin above and below the letter. On folios 1v through 8v, the left side of the capital is filled in with gold. With the exception of the five decorated pages discussed below, after folio 8v the use of gold in capital letters that begin new sections of the text is limited to folios 19r, 19v, 69r, 75v, 79r, and 97r.

Following the customary practice, the entire border area of the first page of the manuscript is decorated. A vine with leaves and flowers in brown, red, green, violet, and originally gold, circles the top, right, and bottom margins. Only light brown traces of the original gold leaves remain. Along the left margin a large gold capital I, outlined in blue with swirls enclosing green, red, and blue cruciform designs, extends eight lines in height. On the left, the ends of the letter connect to the border design, which culminates at the top in a small green dragon with a protruding red tongue. The top half of a nude human figure astride the dragon has disappeared, probably owing to the friction of pages rubbing together. The nine lines that introduce the first prayer are written in red, adding to the attractiveness of the page. Nonetheless, the page has a faded appearance and has sustained considerable damage. The remnant of the Biblioteca Nacional stamp is visible in two places in the right margin.

Floral designs and drolleries in vivid shades of gold, green, red, and blue richly adorn the left margin of five other pages that contain the beginning of different holy offices. The style of the designs on folios 31v, 41v, 44r, 53v, and 58v is similar, but there is no correlation between the illustrations and the content of the pages. On folio 31v, a nude, bird-like figure with hind legs, a long tail, a multicolored wing, and a human face with shoulder-length hair tops the marginal decoration. Folio 41v has an initial *I* seven lines high and a *D* two lines high that intertwine with marginal floral decoration. The page also contains a capital *S* in gold on a blue curvilinear design with a fine red outline, a blue *E* with red decoration, plus several words or lines in red that complete the colorful appearance of the page. Folio 44r has a similar floral decoration in the margin, plus two decorated capitals two lines high and an initial *O* four lines high that begins the Office of the Nails. Folio 53v displays the back of a small male figure, wearing green pants and a reddish-brown shirt, standing on a flower. His face and raised right hand are very brown and his head is topped by a yellow, brimmed hat. Two figures appear among the decoration of folio 58v. In mid-page, a green animal standing upright on two legs shows the profile of an expressive, open-mouthed human face. The beast wears a pointed gold and red cap that matches a cape around his upper body. A winged green dragon with a dolphin-like face appears at the top of the column.

The Edition

The edition tries to meet the needs of as wide a range of readers as possible. In the first place, since there are no other manuscripts or editions of Sor Constanza's prayer book, and since the codex dates from the time of the author, the edition offers a faithful representation of the contents of the manuscript. At the same time, certain alterations have been made in order to provide a readily comprehensible text for the modern reader.

To insure the highest possible level of accuracy, the transcription was done in several stages. The initial transcription, made using an enlarged copy from the microfilm of the codex, was corrected against the original manuscript in the National Library in Madrid. Subsequently, Dr. Heanon Wilkins also read the corrected version against the original codex. In addition, Dr. Gabriel O'Donnell, O.P., the religion consultant, read the transcription and compared the Latin sections with a copy from the microfilm. We then discussed and resolved any differences or problems. Textual corrections and legible marginal insertions that appear to be in the same hand as the text are incorporated into the text and indicated in the notes. Illegible or partially legible marginal notes and those in a later hand are found only in the notes. Whenever possible, letters cropped in the margins are supplied in brackets. There are instances where words or entire lines have been erased and other wording inserted in their place, or the space has been filled with decorative designs, rendering the previous content undecipherable.

Some editorial modifications of the text have been made to maintain consistency in usage and to afford greater ease in reading the devotionary. The ampersand is transcribed as *e*, but *e* and *et* are maintained as they appear in the text. Prefixes or suffixes that are at times separated are joined, for example, *des-*, *in-*, and *-mente*. The preposition *a*, often written as part of the following word, has been transcribed as a separate word to avoid confusion: *avestir > a vestir*. Other prepositions are also separated from the following words: *dela > de la*. The use of *u* and *v* and *i*, *y*, and *j* has been standardized to reflect modern usage. The different forms of *s* have not been indicated; however, missing cedillas on *c* before *a*, *o*, or *u* have been supplied. Modern capitalization, punctuation, and accentuation are employed. Long passages are divided into paragraphs for the sake of clarity. Direct address and quotations are indicated by quotation marks in order to highlight the dramatic nature of the text. The stanzas of Latin hymns in the manuscript are written continuously, beginning with illuminated capitals and with periods indicating the end of the lines. In the edition, they are presented in stanza form. When a folio ends with a divided word, the whole word, with an oblique indicating the point of division, comes before the brackets containing the folio number.

Whenever possible, abbreviations have been resolved, restoring the full spelling. While abbreviations are not uncommon in this text, neither are they found in great abundance. Abbreviations at the end of a word, i.e., suspensions, are infrequent, the most common being the final nasal in words like *do(n)*, *no(n)*, *ni(n)*, or in plural verbs like *aya(n)*. Suspensions also occur in certain religious terms such as *kyriel(eison)*, *laud(abilis)*, *p(salmo)*, and *v(erso)*. Abbreviations within the word are much more common and follow normal patterns, with suppression of a nasal occurring most often, for example, *a(n)i(m)a*, *com(m)o*, *om(n)e*, *domi(n)go*, *s(an)cto*, and *gr(an)t*. Other frequent contractions are: omission of *r* or *r* plus vowel, for example, *vi(r)tud*, *nonb(ra)do*, *lág(ri)mas*; omisson of *ue* or *ui*, for example, *q(ue)*, *n(ue)stro*, *q(ui)*, *chiq(ui)to*; and omission of letters following *p*, for example, *p(ro)phecía*, *p(ro)pter*, *p(ar)a*, *p(re)ciosa*, *p(ri)mero*. Certain frequently used religious terms are nearly always abbreviated, for example, *m(isericord)ia*, *Chr(ist)e*, *Ih(es)u*, *gl(or)ia*, *gl(ori)osa*, *b(e)n(edictu)s*, *s(upe)r*, *d(omi)ne*, *sp(irit)u*, *s(an)c(t)o*, *an(tiphan)a*, *all(eluy)a*, and *p(salmu)s*.

The footnotes are of several types:

1. The paleographic notes describe changes and interlinear or marginal additions. Cases of difficult reading due to faded ink, ink blots, deteriorated pages, erasures, and changed letters or words are included only when the reading is unclear. Other paleographic information is included in the introduction.

2. Definitions are given for Spanish words that are unknown in modern Spanish or have a different form or meaning in modern usage. The Index of Linguistic Citations indicates the first appearance of all Spanish words that have been defined in the notes.

3. Latin words are annotated most often to supply a more complete or more grammatically correct form in order to facilitate understanding.

4. Details are given of persons mentioned in the text.

5. The sources of scriptural, liturgical, and devotional materials are noted. The Index of Scriptural Citations arranges biblical references according to the books of the Bible in which they are found and indicates the pages of the text where they occur. When it seems clear, however, that a citation is from a liturgical source, the biblical origin of the wording is not annotated. For example, the Response on folio 35v is used on the fourth Sunday in Advent at Matins, and consequently the biblical source of the opening words, "Canite tuba in Sion" (Joel 2:15) is not noted. Likewise, biblical echoes and fragments are often not pointed out in order to avoid an undue proliferation of notes that could distract the reader. For example, the following section from folio 37r contains at least three additional references:

. . . *Montes Israel, ramos vestros* [Ezekiel 36:8] expandite et florete et fructus facite. **P.** *Prope est et iam veniet* [Ezekiel 36:8] dies Domini. ℣. Rorate, celi, de super et nubes pluant iustum, apperiatur terra et germinet Salvatorem. **P.** Prope est. **Leccio vi**. Ita Dominus est tecum ut sit in corde tuo et sit in utero tuo, adimpleat mentem tuam, adimpleat ventrem tuum, procedat formosus de utero tuo, *tamquam sponsus de thalamo suo*. *Egrediatur* [Psalm 18:6] rex ex intimo ventre tuo, *tamquam sponsus de cubili suo* [Joel 2:16], procedat princeps ex aula regali . . .

Also not annotated are the numerous examples of abbreviated liturgical and devotional formulae, a common practice in books of the Divine Office and in prayer books.

6. Common orthographic changes are not annotated, but are described below. Spelling changes are generally included in the notes only to avoid confusion between different possible words, for example, *fiel/hiel*.

Orthography

Although orthography is somewhat inconsistent in both the Spanish and the Latin portions of the text, a number of changes are fairly regular. In addition to abbreviations and fusion and separation of words mentioned above, frequent usages in Spanish are: the addition or elimination of an initial *h*; *f* written for initial *h*; interchange of nasals; interchange of final *d* and *t*; omission of final *s* at the end of a word preceding a word beginning with *s*, for example, *tu santos*; omission of *a* before a word starting with *a*; and alternation of unaccented vowels, for example, *conplida/cumplida*. Forms of the present participle normally end in *te*, for example, *trayente* for *trayendo* or *stante* for *estando*. Verbs in the future subjunctive are regularly apocopated, for example, *fuer* or *pudier*. A number of spelling conventions are apparent in the Latin: *ci* for *ti* and vice versa, *e* for *ae* and *oe*, *e* for *et*, *h* is added or omitted, *ch* for *h*, *p* added to *mn*, *f* for *ph* and vice versa, consonants doubled or made single, *x* for *s* or *ss*, *i* for *e* and vice versa, *o* for *u* and vice versa, *nt* for *nct*, *t* for *d* and vice versa, *ct* for *th* or *t*, *n* for *m* especially in final position and vice versa, *dj* for *j*, *n* for *dn*, *mm* for *nm*. Prefixes like *ad* and *in* xxii

are regularly separated from the root of compound verbs and occasionally from nouns.

mea et non ſum oigna uiore alti
tuomem oelh pre multituomem un
quitatis mee quomaʒ irritam ira
tui ʒ malii oraʒ te feci. Capitulo. x
Jhu miſericie mei, poʒ uirtuo ðl
oolor oonque te aɾjroiſte
te tus orciplos el uicacs ðf
pues te oena muy iſtigoō te apaʒ
taſte oellos mucho enſanguſtiaoo oo
temoʒ oela muerte. Oraſte al paoʒe oi
ʒienoo. Triſtis e aia mea uſque ao moʒ
tem. Seoioʒ poʒ mi tu eſclaua. Soliʒe
amꝛiae. Enel monte oliueti tanto oof
trenioo fueſte, yo te ſuplico anſi oomo
tu eres uioa perpetua. me ðf gracia
que ðfee moʒa poʒ tu amoʒ ʒ me ari
coir oelas oonuerſaciones oaiioſas
a mi aia. E oe los negoeios oel mun
oo enque me yo oeupo. Oomo traſte
aſanit pablo oe perſeguir tus cɾiaiio
Jhu miſericie mei poʒ. Cap. xi.

Madrid, Biblioteca Nacional, MS 7495, folio 5r

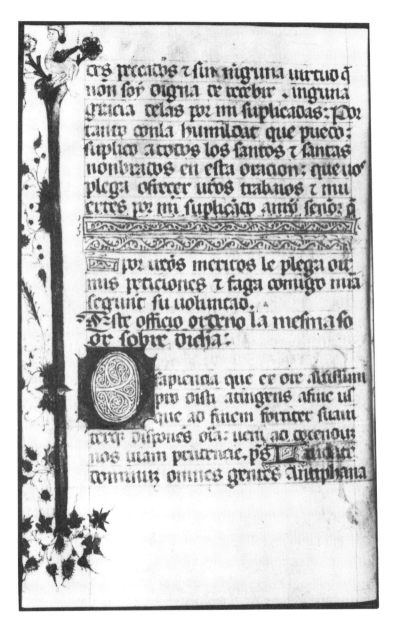

çrs preçadõs ⁊ sin ninguna uirtuo q̃
non soy digna de reçebir . ninguna
graçia delas por mi suplicadas: por
tanto conla humildat que puedo:
suplico atodos los santos ⁊ santas
nonbrados en esta oraçion: que uos
plega ofreçer uros trabaios ⁊ mu
ertes por mi suplicaçio ami senõr q̃

por uros meritos le plega oir
mis petiçiones ⁊ faga comigo mia
segunt su uoluntad.
Este officio ordeno la mesma so
or sobre dicha:

O sapiencia que de ore altissimi
pro disti atingens afine us
que ad finem fortiter suaui
terq̃ dispones oia: ueni ad docendur
nos uiam prudencie. ps̄ Laudate
dominu̷ omnes gentes Antiphana

Madrid, Biblioteca Nacional, MS 7495, folio 31v

Constanza de Castilla

Libro de devociones y oficios

Esta oraçión que se sigue conpuso una soror de la orden de Sancto Domingo de los Predicadores, la qual es grant pecadora. E ruega a quantas personas la rezaren que le den parte de su devoçión. E suplica a Nuestro Señor que la faga partiçionera de sus mereçimientos. Dévese dezir esta oraçión ante de la comunión.

Capítulo primero. Ihesu, miserere mei, por virtud de la tu sancta encarnaçión, quando te plogo[1] desçender del seno del Padre en el sagrario de la Virgen Gloriosa tomando de sus entrañas vestidura de omne,[2] estoviste allí nueve meses ençerado. Señor, pues por mí tu esclava plogo a ti, verbo de Dios, tanto humillarte a vestir tan pobre vestidura, yo suplico a ti por la grandeza de la tu humildat que me libres del pecado de sobervia,[3] en la qual muchas ve/zes [1v] caygo por mi culpa. E dame virtud de humildat conplida[4] por que[5] yo conosca la grant miseria mía commo don. Quia ego sum pulvis, cinis, vermis et non

---

[1] *plogo*: ant. preterite of *placer*, "it pleased," but also includes the idea of an exertion of will.

[2] *omne*: ant. *hombre*.

[3] *la* before *sobervia* erased and replaced by short curved line.

[4] *conplida*: ant. *cumplida*.

[5] *por que*: separation between the two words is maintained when the meaning indicates purpose, equivalent to *para que*.

homo, opprobrium hominum et abieccio plebbis.[6]

Capítulo segundo. Ihesu, miserere mei, por virtud del tu sancto nasçimiento, quando poderosamente glorioso saliste del vientre virginal cerrado, te nos[7] diste Dios et omne por nos librar de la muerte, a que éramos obligados. Señor, pues por mí tu esclava te plogo nascer en logar tan pobre et desechado, yo te adoro Dios et omne excelente puesto en el pesebre sobre seno resfriado chiquito en poca ropa enbuelto entre dos alimañas. Señor, yo te suplico, por el tu nascimiento sancto, que alinpies mi coraçón de todo odio e rencor e me des virtud de caridad ordenada que la yo obre commo sancto Do/mingo,[8] [2r] nuestro padre.

Capítulo tercero. Ihesu, miserere mei, por virtud del sancto nonbre Ihesu que te fue nonbrado al octavo día quando te plogo ser circuncidado commo pecador, en commo[9] tú fueses Dios e omne, la tu preciosa sangre començaste derramar por nuestra redenpçión, lloraste lágrimas con dolor de la nueva llaga que reçebiste cunpliendo la ley a que non eras obligado. Señor, pues tan tierno padesciste por mí tu esclava, yo te suplico me des gracia quel tu nonbre Ihesu sea escripto en mi coraçón commo en el de sancto Ynacio.[10]

---

[6] Psalm 21:7 plus *pulvis cinis* from Genesis 18:27. Used at the hour of Prime in Lent and as a tract for Passion Sunday. Latin biblical references and quotations are from *Biblia Sacra Iuxta Vulgatam Versionem* (Stuttgart: Deutsche Bibelgesellschaft, 1983).

[7] *cerrado te nos*: possibly in a different hand, in dark ink with *nos* extending into margin, written over a previous word.

[8] *Santo Domingo de Guzmán*: founder of the Order of Preachers, born in Caleruega in Old Castile c. 1170, characterized by certain virtues, especially austerity and charity. Reputedly, he tried as a youth to alleviate hunger in his province by selling his books.

[9] *en commo*: ant. *como*, here used with *fueses* as the equivalent of the gerund *siendo*.

[10] St. Ignatius: Bishop of Antioch at the beginning of the second century, second Apostolic father, characterized by extreme passion and zeal in his epistles to the churches in response to Trajan's persecutions. When the emperor demanded that he identify himself, Ignatius replied that he was the one who bore Christ in his breast. He was killed by wild beasts in the Roman arena. His

Capítulo quarto. Ihesu, miserere mei, por virtud de la sanctíssima presentación que la Virgen tu madre fizo en el templo, conplidos quarenta días del tu naçimiento, non seiendo nesçesario, cumplió la ley. Te ofreció en las manos del justo Simeón que te mucho desea/va [2v] ver, sabiendo que eras el Mexías prometido. E desque[11] te vido, con grant reverencia, alegría et devoción te recibió diciendo: "Nunc dimictis servum tuum, Domine, secundum verbum tuum in pace."[12] Señor, yo te suplico que ansí cunplas mis buenos deseos commo a este justo.

Capítulo quinto. Ihesu, miserere mei, por la obediencia que conpliste el primero año del tu nascimiento quando la Gloriosa et Joseph fueron contigo a tiera de Egipto por miedo de Erodes,[13] donde siete años visquiste[14] desterado, peregrino, pobre, encogido, menospreciado, avergonçado, en los tienpos de tu viaje a la ida e tornada sofriste cansançio, fanbre,[15] sed, frío, et calor, tú mucho tierno de pocos días, la Gloriosa seiendo donzella delicada, et pobre Josep viejo. Inpotente, menguado[16] de las provisiones necesarias, pasaste la grande aspereza del desi/erto. [3r] Señor, pues por mí tu esclava te plogo fuir del rey mortal, commo tú mesmo sacaste el pueblo de Ysrael del poder de Pharaón, yo te suplico, por la grandeza del tu poder, que fuerçes gravitatem meam[17] que me estorva tu servicio. E dame virtud que yo cunpla tus mandamientos e los de mi orden por que yo sea obediente a ti, commo san Pedro quando fue a Roma a morir en cruz.

Capítulo vi. Ihesu, parçe michi, por el santo sacramento del

Epistle to the Romans "became a sort of martyr's manual" (Lightfoot 1, 1, p. 38). His teaching insists on the dual human and divine natures of Christ, a theme also occurring in this chapter and throughout the prayer book.

[11] *desque*: ant. *después que*.

[12] Luke 2:29. Used each night at Compline and on 2 February, the feast of the Purification of the Blessed Virgin Mary.

[13] *Erodes*: initial *H* interlinear in different hand.

[14] *visquiste*: ant. preterite of *vivir*.

[15] *fanbre*: ant. *hambre*.

[16] *menguado*: ant. *falto*.

[17] *gravitatem meam*: used frequently to refer to sins or the burden of sins in the writings of church fathers and in prayers of devotion.

baptismo que reçebiste quando santificaste las aguas de la fuente Jordán e les diste virtud regenerativa, el Spíritu Sancto descendió sobre ti en figura de paloma. El Padre en boz te dixo: "Hic est filius meus dilectus in quo michi bene conplacuit."[18] E sannt Juan con temor non te osava tañer,[19] lançándose a tus pies con grant reverençia conosciendo que eras Dios, dixo: "Sanc/tifica [3v] me, Salvator." Señor, yo te suplico que te plega lavar mi ánima de las muchas manzillas que tiene e tires de mi coraçón toda orrura[20] carnal e me des virtud de linpieza conplida, commo diste a Santiago el Justo[21] por que yo goce de ti.

Capítulo seteno. Ihesu, miserere mei, por el trabajo que pasaste quando quarenta días e noches ayunaste en el desierto sin comer nin bever, apartado de la vista de tu madre, en fin plógote padesçer fanbre e sed, ansí commo omne verdadero por mayor mérito quesiste ser tentado del enemigo. E tú, rey, le venciste por tu propio poder, e menospreciaste commo aquél que por tu ordenança avía seído del cielo deribado. Señor, pues por mí tu esclava te plogo sofrir estos trabajos, yo te adoro Dios e omne en el desierto vençedor e te suplico me des virtud de firme constançia por que yo sienpre vensca las tentaciones del enemigo e[22] [4r] del mundo e[23] de la carne, commo libraste los tres niños en las flamas del forno.[24]

Capítulo viij. Ihesu, miserere mei, por virtud de las muy poderosas,

---

[18] Matthew 3:17.

[19] *taner*: *tocar*.

[20] *orrura*: filth, superfluity, also ant. *horror*.

[21] *Santiago el Justo*: also known as the Less or the Younger, son of Alpheus. According to Eusebius, the church historian, James was holy from his mother's womb. He did not drink wine or eat food that had life in it, nor did he bathe, anoint himself with oil, or allow a razor to touch his head. He was called "the Just" because of his great justice and intercessions on behalf of the people.

[22] *e*: uncertain reading because of ink blot.

[23] *e* added interlinear.

[24] *tres niños*: Daniel 3; Shadrach, Meshach, and Abednego preferred to be cast into a fiery furnace rather than worship the golden image made by King Nebuchadnezzar. The three youths miraculously emerged untouched by the fire.

excelentes e maravillosas obras que obraste, grandíssimos trabajos que tú sofriste en treynta e tres años que en este mundo visquiste.[25] Señor, por virtut de tus proprias obras te suplico tires de mí el pecado de la accidia que mucho en mí regina[26] e me estorva tus obras de continuo, e ordenes que te sirva con diligencia, commo sannt Josep[27] e santa Marta.[28]

Capítulo ix. Ihesu, miserere mei, por el trabajo que tomaste el jueves de la cena, quando dando enxenplo[29] a nos con humildad de rodillas te pusiste a lavar los pies de tus deçiplos, e después con entrañable amor instituiste el sancto sacra/mento [4v] del tu cuerpo glorioso en memoria de la sagrada passión tuya. E diste plenario poderío a los sacerdotes para lo consag[r]ar.[30] E hordenaste manjar espiritual a todos los fieles que dignamente te recibieren por que te ayan en esta vida en memoria e conpanía. Señor, humillmente suplico a ti, que de los pecadores fazes justos, te plega alinpiar et justificarme commo tú sabes a mí es neçesario segunt mis graves e muchos errores e la grandeza de mi maldat, e la grant frialdat et apartamiento de tu memoria que en mí es, commo obraste en sancta Catalina de Sena.[31] Ca yo, grave pecadora,

---

[25] *visquiste*: + *principa[l]mente e[l] miercol[es] quando [te] despedi[ste] de la glo[rio]sa e ma[ ]rias q[ ] te queri[an] desci[ ] muer[te]* in margin.

[26] *regina*: read *reina*.

[27] St. Joseph, the carpenter, is an example of willingness to work with his hands and minister to the child Jesus. Devotion to St. Joseph, husband of Mary and foster father of Jesus, was introduced into the medieval tradition in the twelfth century by St. Bernard of Clairvaux.

[28] St. Martha, sister of Mary and Lazarus, served and waited on Jesus, an example of active works in contrast to Mary's contemplation. See Luke 10:38-42 and John 11 and 12:1-2.

[29] *enxenplo*: ant. *ejemplo*.

[30] *consag[r]ar*: letters that appear in brackets are editorial insertions.

[31] St. Catherine of Siena, born 1347, Dominican tertiary, example from childhood of penitence, self-denial, virtue, and heroism. Cared for lepers during the plague of 1374. In a vision, she saw rays of light coming from the wounds of the crucified Jesus to the same places on her body. At her request, the stigmata were visible only to her. She has been a model and patron of Third Order Dominicans.

non soy digna de te reçebir nin de alçar mis ojos ante la tu poderosa majestad, e conoçiendo mis muchos peccados confiesso: Peccavi et super numerum arene maris,[32] multiplicata sunt peccata [5r] mea, et non sum digna videre altitudinem celi, pre multitudinem iniquitatis mee quoniam irritavi iram tuam et malum coram te feci.[33]

Capítulo x. Ihesu, miserere mei, por virtud del dolor con que te despediste de tus deçiplos el jueves después de cena muy afligido, te apartaste dellos mucho ensangustiado[34] con temor de la muerte. Oraste al padre diziendo: "Tristis est anima mea usque ad mortem."[35] Señor, por mí tu esclava, solus et anxiatus en el monte Oliveti tanto constreñido fueste, yo te suplico, ansí commo tú eres vida perpetua, me des graçia que desee morir por tu amor e me ariedre[36] de las conversaçiones dañosas a mi ánima e de los negoçios del mundo en que me yo ocupo, commo tiraste a sannt Pablo[37] de perseguir tus cristianos.

Capítulo xi. Ihesu, miserere mei, por [5v] el merescimiento de la virtuosa oraçión que tú feciste[38] quando con grande humildat posiste las rodillas, el tu reverendo rostro a par de la terra, con grande agonía e aflicçión de la carne dixiste: "Pater, si posible est transeat a me calix

---

[32] *maris*: + interlinear *e*.

[33] *Peccavi . . . feci*: response at Matins during the First Week after Octave of Pentecost.

[34] *ensangustiado*: ant. *angustiado*.

[35] Matthew 26:38. Sung on Passion Sunday by three persons representing Christ, the narrator, and the crowd.

[36] *ariedre*: from *arredrar*, "to move away, turn away."

[37] Before his conversion, the great apostle, St. Paul, had been instructed and charged to persecute Christians. Paul was a consenting witness to the execution of Stephen, the first Christian martyr. On his way to Damascus to actively participate in the persecution of Christians, Paul was struck down and blinded by a great light from heaven. At the same time, Jesus spoke, rebuking Paul and telling him to await his instructions. Following his confession of faith to Jesus and his subsequent baptism, Paul's sight was restored. After his conversion to Christianity, Paul was distinguished for his great work as an apostle and missionary of God.

[38] *feciste*: ant. *hiciste*.

iste."[39] Señor, pues por mí tu esclava sofriste tan grande pavor, yo te suplico me des virtud de esfuerço en la ora temerosa de mi fin quando mi espíritu será puesto en estrecha batalla propter varias temptaciones diaboli. E plégate arredrar de mi entendimiento todas dubdas e malos pensamientos en que mi naturaleza revesada se pueda ocupar, ca propter peto cum David: Illumina occllos meos ne umquam obdormiam in morte; ne quando dicat inimicus meus: Prevalui adversus eam.[40]

Capítulo doze. Ihesu, miserere mei, por virtud [6r] del terrible trabajo que tú passaste quando, pensando en la[41] muerte que avías de sofrir, sudaste gotas de sangre afligido por la batalla que la sensualidat avía con el spíritu. E tú, rey poderoso, venciste diziendo: "Pater, non sicut ego volo set sicut tu."[42] Señor, pues por mí tu esclava padesciste tan soberano temor, yo te suplico, por virtud de aquella preçiosa sang[r]e que tú por mí sudaste, me quieras consolar quando mi espíritu será puesto en grant conflicto e confusión porque mis malas obras serán declaradas ante ti e mi mesma conciencia acusará mis fechos e mis enemigos clamarán a ti que les fagas de mí justicia. Señor, en aquella ora[43] plega a tu misericordia mostrárteme Dios e omne piadoso, commo a santa Catalina martir quando en la cárcel la visitaste e sanaste sus llagas.[44]

---

[39] Matthew 26:39.
[40] Psalm 12:4b-5a, used as the first nocturn of Sunday Matins.
[41] *la*: + *orrible* in margin.
[42] Matthew 26:39, used on Passion Sunday.
[43] *ora*: initial *h* added interlinear.
[44] St. Catherine of Alexandria defied the Emperor Maxentius's order to worship pagan idols. According to legend, after a debate in which she defeated fifty scholars, the Emperor had Catherine stripped, beaten with iron rods so that her entire body was covered with wounds, and thrown into a dungeon for twelve days without food or light. Heavenly angels healed her wounds with ointments, and a dove brought her nourishment to sustain her body. Later, God visited Catherine face to face in the prison in order to comfort her. The Church celebrates her on 25 November, the date the virgin martyr was beheaded. St. Catherine, St. Mary Magdalene, and St. Cecilia were the three protectors or patrons of the Order chosen by St. Dominic.

10

Capítulo xiij. Ihesu, miserere mei, por el trabajo que tomaste [6v] quando con temor de la muerte así commo omne sintiendo soledat despertaste tus deziplos diziendo: "Non potuistis una ora vigilare mecum? Vigilate e orate quoniam tribulacio proxima est et non est qui adiuvet."[45] Esto les dezías tú, Señor mío, rogándoles que te aconpañasen por que Judas non te fallase solo, que estava aparejando gente de armas para prender a ti poderoso Dios, cordero manso. Señor, pues por mí tu esclava te plogo padesçer tan estrecha soledat, yo te suplico, a la ora que mis fuerças falleçerán[46] e mi coraçón será rasgado con dolor de la muerte, tú me quieras visitar por tu gracia e despiertes mi ánima e non la dexes dormir en pecado; quando oviere[47] de pasar deste valle de lágrimas non esté obstinada nin adormeçida en ningunt eror,[48] mas despierta en fervor e amor tuyo de se ir a ti, mi Salvador, que eres vida. E non te deleitas en la per/dición [7r] de los malos.

Capítulo xiiij. Ihesu, parçe michi, por el trabajo que pasaste quando con soberana obediençia ygualaste tu voluntat con la de Dios, pudieras dezir:[49] "Padre, pues neçesario es a salvaçión del humanal linaje quod unus moriatur homo pro populo ne tota gens pereat,[50] tú quieres que yo satisfaga sus debdas,[51] la tu sentençia en mí sea executada, yo lo acepto. E te pido que me ayudes e non me desanpares en esta lid por que yo sea vençedor e reconcilie contigo a Adam e a sus fijos. E non mea voluntas set tua fiat."[52] Acabada la[53] oración, el angel tu servidor con reverençia

---

[45] *Non . . . orate*: Matthew 26:40-41; *quoniam . . . adiuvet*: Psalm 21:12.

[46] *falleçerán*: in the margin in a different hand.

[47] *oviere*: future subjunctive of *haber*.

[48] Additional *r* added interlinear to convert *eror* to *error*.

[49] *pudieras dezir*: the imperfect subjunctive is used here to indicate the hypothetical nature of the following words. Chapter xxxii uses the conditional for a similar purpose.

[50] *quod . . . pereat*: John 11:50. The line is used by Caiaphus to justify Jesus's death; here used by Jesus for a different purpose.

[51] *debdas*: ant. *deudas*.

[52] *E . . . fiat*: Luke 22:42b. Reference to the angel in the following line is also from the same chapter of Luke.

[53] *la* interlinear.

te conortó.[54] O rex inmortalis e amoroso, yo te adoro, vençedor de la carne, que por dar a mí vida obedeçiste la muerte. Señor mío, por esta sentencia tan dura que por mí tu esclava conpliste, te suplico que ansí iguales mi voluntad con [7v] la tuya, commo ygualaste la tuya con la del Padre. E en la estrema ora mía, quando veré la espantosa vista de los enemigos que tomarán lid contra mí por los gravíssimos pecados que yo cometí, a la tu misericordia plega en tienpo de tan grant espanto enbiarme consolaçión angélica, pues eres poderoso, por que yo pueda dezir: Factus es michi, Domine, mi refugium et Deus meus in adiuctorium mee.[55]

Capítulo quinze. Ihesu, miserere mei, por el trabajo que pasaste quando con entrañable amor te ofreciste e diste a los judíos que te venían prender. E tú, rey perdurable, conpliendo nuestra redenpción te llegaste a ellos, llamando amigo a Judas abaxaste tu excelente cabeça, dístele tu preciosa boca a que te diese paz.[56] E dixiste [8r] a los judíos dos vezes con mansedunbre: "Quem queritis ego sum."[57] E por defensión de los tuyos dixiste: "Si ergo me queritis sinite hos abire."[58] Bendicho[59] seas tú, Señor poderoso, que por mí tu esclava te ofreciste a la muerte, yo suplico a ti, que numquam cessem[60] querentibus te, que me des virtud que sienpre mi coraçón esté atado contigo toda mi vida commo estovo sannt Juan[61] en todos los actos e tormentos que padeciste fasta[62] el sepulcro.

Capítulo xvj. Ihesu, miserere mei, por el trabajo que pasaste quando los judíos desonrradamente te prendieron a la ora de los matines, muy furiosamente sin ninguna cortesía te echaron la soga a la garganta e ataron tus sagradas manos atrás. Con toda crueldat mesaron tus

---

[54] *conortó*: *confortó, consoló.*
[55] *adiuctorium*: + illegible word of 3-4 letters in margin; *mee*: read *meum.*
[56] The meeting with Judas is described in Matthew 26:49-50.
[57] Combination of John 18:4b and 5b.
[58] John 18:8b.
[59] *Bendicho*: ant. *bendito.*
[60] *cessem*: uncertain reading.
[61] *Juan* changed to *Iohan.*
[62] *fasta*: + *te pone[r en]* in the margin.

12

cabellos. E estirando unos atrás e otros adelante te levaron a casa del obispo Anas [8v] e delante dél te acusaron[63] muchas injurias. Ca el su moço Malco, a quien tú sanaste la oreja, te dio una gran bofetada en tu esplendíssimo rostro tan fuerte que atronó tu maxilla e te fizo señal diziendo: "Sic respondes pontifici?"[64] E tú, rey del çielo, con sentimiento del grande dolor dixiste: "Si male locutus sum, testimonium perhibe de malo; si atem[65] bene cur me cedis."[66] Bendicho seas tú, Señor mío, Dios eterno, que por mí tu esclava lo sofriste. Por ende, Señor, yo te suplico me des virtud que sufra por tu reverençia e amor todas dolientias e dolores e trabajos, ansí corporales commo espirituales, commo sufri[ó][67] el fuego sannt Lorenço puesto en las parillas sobre las brasas.[68]

Capítulo xvii. Ihesu, miserere mei, por la soledat que pasaste quando fuiste[69] desanparado de tus dizípulos e te viste en [9r] poder de tus enemigos que te perseguían con vituperios, escarnios, crueldades sin número, diziendo falsos testimonios. Señor, pues por mí tu esclava lo sofriste, yo te soplico me des virtud que yo sienpre por tu reverentia e amor cesse de te[70] ofender, e alinpia mi coraçón de los pecados de enbidia e maliçia, que en ellos ligeramente peco, e confesando digo: "Peccata mea, Domine, sicut sagite infixa sunt in me, set antequam

---

[63] *acusaron*: possibly an error for *causaron*; the *s* seems to be written over a previous letter.

[64] John 18:22b. Words spoken by a Roman officer, here put into the mouth of Malchus. In John 18:10, the apostle Peter cut off the ear of Malchus, a servant of the High Priest Caiaphas, who had gone to the Garden of Gethsemane to seize Jesus. Annas was the father-in-law of Caiaphas. Luke 22:51 relates the cure by Jesus.

[65] *atem*: *autem*.

[66] John 18:23.

[67] *sufri[ó]* in the margin.

[68] St. Laurence, deacon of the Roman Church, was martyred c. 258 by being slowly roasted over a gridiron.

[69] *fuiste*: *i* erased

[70] *reverentia . . . te* plus *o* of *ofender* written over a previous erasure and therefore difficult to read, *de te o* extends into margin.

vulnera generent in me sana me, Domine, medicamento penitencie, Deus."

Capítulo xviij. Ihesu, parçe michi, ansí commo perdonaste a sannt Pedro que te negó tres vezes, tú le acataste[71] con ojos de piedat, semejablemente[72] te suplico me acates con ojos de misericordia pues soy aquella que muchas vezes te ha[73] negado e fecho grandes ofen/sas [9v] por mi maldat. Ansí mesmo he fallescido[74] tu fe e esperança; conosçiendo mis muchos errores confiesso: Tribularem si ne sciren misericordias tuas, Domine, qui dixisti: "Nollo mortem pecatoris set ut magis convertatur e vivat,"[75] qui cananeam et publicanum[76] vocasti ad penitenciam, Magdalen[77] remisisti peccata multa et Petrum lacrimantem sucepisti misericors Deus.

Capítulo xix. Ihesu, miserere mei, por la desonra que sufriste quando los judíos, abiltadamente[78] renpujándote a una parte e a otra, dándote enpellones, con grant vituperio blasfemando de ti, te levaron a casa de Caifas. E te preguntó si eras fijo de Dios. E desque tú con omildat respondiste: "Ego sum,"[79] él con malicia ronpió sus vestiduras diziendo: "Blasfemavit."[80] E con su favor[81] escupieron tu cara, que es gloria santorum, mesaron tu cabeça gloriosa; [10r] unos dieron golpes en tu pescueço, otros palmadas en tu rostro, que es refeçio angelorum,

---

[71] *acataste*: ant. "looked carefully, contemplated."

[72] *semejablemente*: ant. *semejantemente*, "thus," "similarly."

[73] *ha*: second letter altered, unclear if it should read *he* or *ha*.

[74] *fallescido*: ant. "failed to keep."

[75] *Nollo . . . vivat*: similar in words and ideas to Ezechiel 18:23 and 32 and Ezechiel 33:11.

[76] *cananeam*: reference to the Canaanite woman, in Matthew 15:22-28, whose great faith so impressed Jesus that he cured her daughter; *publicanum*: for the call of Levi, the tax collector (also called Matthew), see Matthew 9:9-13, Mark 2:13-17, and Luke 5:27-32.

[77] *Magdalen*: a final *a* added above the line.

[78] *abiltadamente*: ant. "insultingly, ignominiously."

[79] Mark 14:62.

[80] Matthew 26:65.

[81] *favor*: possibly Latin influence meaning "support" or "approval."

diziendo: "Profetiza quis est qui te percusit."[82] Señor, pues por mí tu esclava lo sofriste, yo te suplico me des virtud de paciencia conplida con que yo sufra todas las injurias,[83] daños, escarnios por ti, commo diste fortaleza al apóstol sancto Thomé quando fue abierto por las entrañas,[84] e me libres del pecado de la yra e de toda crueldat por los merescimientos de sannt P[ ]um e sannt Feliciam.[85]

Capítulo xx. Ihesu, miserere mei, por la angustia que passaste a la ora de la prima quando Pilato contra justiçia dio falsa sentençia que fueses açotado. Señor, yo te suplico me libres accecitate[86] cordis e tiniebla de que mi entendimiento está lleno. E dame graçia que yo juzgue justiçia [10v] derecha tal que plega a ti; e si fuer[87] menester, que yo muera por la tu justiçia e verdat, commo sannt Juan bautista.[88]

Capítulo xxj. Ihesu, miserere mei, por las penas que sofriste quando reçebiste los crudos açotes con graves dolores, tu cuerpo despojado, llagado de espantosas e crueles llagas dando de ti abondosa sangre por que se cumpliese en ti la propheçía de Isayas: "Quis est iste qui venit de Eoden, tinctis vestibus de Bosrra?"[89] Señor, pues por mí tu esclava lo sofriste, yo te adoro e te suplico por mereçimiento de estas

---

[82] Luke 22:64. Similarly Matthew 26:68.

[83] *injurias*: some letters erased and covered by an abstract swirl. In the margin *inju* in very faint letters.

[84] St. Thomas: The lesson for Matins on 21 December celebrates his evangelizing India and his martyrdom there by being pierced with lances.

[85] Uncertain reading of the first name. Possibly a reference to Saints Primus and Felician (c. 297), Roman Christians who devoted themselves to works of charity. Because of their refusal to sacrifice to Roman gods, they were imprisoned, tortured, and beheaded.

[86] *accecitate*: letters changed and squeezed into the space.

[87] *fuer*: apocopated form of future subjunctive, *fuere*.

[88] St. John, called the Baptist because he administered baptism by water to Jesus and to penitents who had renounced their sins. At the instigation of Herod's wife, John was beheaded because he had said it was unlawful for Herod to marry his brother's wife. For an account of John's death, see Matthew 14:1-2 and Mark 6:14-29.

[89] Isaiah 63:1. *Eoden* should read *Edom*.

llagas amortigües todos mis malos pensamientos e me des fe cumplida[90] commo la diste al ladrón penado en la cruz.

Capítulo xxij. Ihesu, miserere mei, por la desonra que reçebiste quando Pilatos por escarnio te fizo vestir de púrpura commo a omne sin seso e pusieron en tu cabeça corona de espinas agu/das [11r] que traspasaron tu santíssimo celebro cumpliendo la prophecía del rey Salamón: "Filie Iherusalim, venite et videte regem coronatum."[91] E por te más vituperiar con un paño velaron tu faz ques splendor[92] Dei Patris. E escarneçiendo de ti fincadas las rodillas dezían: "Ave, rex Judeorum."[93] E tantos golpes te dieron con la caña que atronaron e desvaneçieron tu exçelente cabeça. E non contentos de estas crueldades, a grandes bozes clamavan: "Crucifige, crucifige eum."[94] E tú, buen Ihesu, así atormentado, muy omilmente[95] lo sufriste todo por mí tu esclava que lo non meresco. Por ende, Señor, yo te suplico, con aquella humildat que puedo, me des virtud que con divida[96] reverençia yo te adore quando te viere en el altar so[97] aquella forma e figura [e] en aquella vista me deleite. Commo santo Thomás dotor, te adoro e contemplo tus [11v] obras.[98]

Capítulo xxiij. Ihesu, miserere mei, por la obediencia que obraste, quando, después que Pilatos fizo preguntas enfengidas, con yprocresía lavó sus manos conosciendo tu inocencia. Después con temor de César[99] dio sentencia que fueses crucificado, la qual sentencia tanto dura con agradable voluntad obedesciste por conplir nuestra rede[m]pçión. Señor,

---

[90] *cumplida*: + *[en] ti* in the margin.
[91] Similar to Song of Solomon 3:11.
[92] *faz*: *z* and *ques* in the margin; *splendor* replaces an erased word.
[93] Matthew 27:29, Mark 15:18, John 19:3.
[94] Mark 15:13, 14; John 19:6.
[95] *omilmente*: *humilmente, humildemente.*
[96] *divida*: i.e., *debida.*
[97] *so*: from Latin *sub*, ant. *debajo de.*
[98] St. Thomas Aquinas (1225-1274), Dominican theologian and Doctor of the Church, insisted on the doctrine of the true presence of Christ in the sacrament of the eucharist.
[99] *Cesar*: + *[o]ra tercia* in the margin.

pues por mí tu esclava negaste a ti mesmo, tú criador seiendo obediente a la criatura, yo te suplico que me libres con tu mano poderosa del pecado de la ypocresía[100] e de todo enfengimiento[101] que dé muerte al ánima, commo libraste a sant Pedro de las aguas de la mar.[102]

Capítulo xxiiij. Ihesu, miserere mei, por el cansancio que pasaste levando la pesada cruz encima de tus onbros,[103] que [12r] non se fartavan tus enemigos de te penar. E fizieron delante ti pregones de falsedat llamándote ladrón, malfechor, enemigo de Dios, tú, seiendo Dios verdadero, por mí tu esclava lo sofriste. Señor, yo te suplico me des virtud que mi lengua sea linpia de toda murmuraçión, e que mis orejas sean sordas a las razones[104] que me provocan a pecar et oigan tus loores[105] e los oficios divinos con diligencia. Gloria, laus et honor tibi sit, rex Christe, redemptor nostre, filii David.

Capítulo xxv. Ihesu, miserere mei, por el grant pesar que sofriste veiendo la dolorosa madre tuya venir en pos de ti, llena de dolor saliendo de la çibdat de Jerusalem. Oíste sus gemidos conosçiendo cómmo yva turbada, ensangustiada. Veiéndote en poder de tus enemigos, [12v] que te levavan a dar muerte de cruz entre dos ladrones, la Señora muy aquexada se apresuró por se llegar a ti con muchas lágrimas e çolloços.[106] E tú, Señor, commo la sintieses, tu coraçón fue agraviado con pesar tanto grande que ovieras a[107] caer en tiera, assí commo omne desfallecido de las fuerças naturales, cansado de muchos tormentos, dolores que toda la noche e día avías soportado non aviendo descanso alguno. Así atormentado con amor natural de fijo, por la consolar bolviste tu rostro a ella, fablaste a las mugeres que la aconpanavan: "Filie Iherusalim, nolite flere super me."[108] E la triste madre desque

---

[100] *ypocresía*: very difficult to read, especially the first three letters.
[101] *enfengimiento*: ant. *fingimiento*.
[102] Matthew 14:28-31.
[103] *onbros*: ant. *hombros*.
[104] *razones*: ant. "words, conversations, opinions."
[105] *loores*: + *de con[tin]uo te bendi[ga] e alab[e]* in the margin.
[106] *çolloços*: i.e., *sollozos*.
[107] *ovieras a* + inf.: ant. *haber de, tener que*.
[108] Luke 23:28.

vido[109] tu cuerpo todo llagado, tu rostro escupido escurecido,[110] tu cabeça
de espinas coronada, una señal negra en tu maxilla, tus ojos apremidos,[111] commo non te podía conoçer pudo preguntar a los judíos:
"¿Qué omne es éste que levades [13r] a matar con tanta priesa e
oprobrio?" E ellos respondían: "Muger, ¿qué preguntas tú? ¿Non
conosçes este omne ser tu fijo Ihesu que se llama rey nuestro?" La
Señora pudo dezir: "Señores, dexadme llegar por que conosca si es él,
que de mi fijo fue escripto: Speciosus forma pre filiis hominum."[112] E
commo non la dexaron llegar a ti, su coraçón fue[113] atormentado de dolor
sin medida. Señor, pues por mí tu esclava te plogo tanto padesçer, a tu
madre tanto atormentar, yo te suplico por su amor me des buena fin.[114]

Capítulo xxvj. Ihesu, miserere mei, por la vergüença que pasaste
quando fueste despojado e quedaste desnudo delante todo el pueblo,
Señor, pues por mí tu esclava diste tu cuerpo a su [13v] suplicio e tus
vestiduras a ser puestas en suertes, yo suplico a la tu conplida proveza[115]
me des graçia que yo por ti[116] menosprecie todas riquezas superfluas.[117]
E me libres de los peccados de cobdiçia e vanagloria por que yo deseche
las vestiduras e apostamientos[118] superfluos de vanidad en que yo te
ofendo, e conosca la desechada miseria mía que la naturaleza me dio e
lo que soy e en que tengo de tornar, [e] en pobreza de espíritu siga a ti,
buen Ihesu, como los apóstoles.

Capítulo xxvij. Ihesu, miserere mei, por los multiplicados dolores
que tú, Señor, padesçiste a la ora de la sesta quando los judíos llenos de

---

109 *vido*: ant. pret. of *ver*.

110 *escurecido*: second *e* added above the line; ant. *oscurecido*.

111 *apremidos*: ant. "lowered, cast down."

112 Psalm 44:3.

113 *fue*: *e* added interlinear in a later hand.

114 *me . . . fin* in darker ink with slightly larger letters, replaces a previous
erasure.

115 *proveza*: metathesized form of *pobreza*.

116 *ti*: + *[de] coraçón* in the margin.

117 *superfluas*: + *[con]plidamente commo las [re]nuncié en [mi] profesión*
in the margin.

118 *apostamientos*: ant. *adornos, atavíos*.

crueldat cruçificaron a ti, Ihesu benigno, non acatando tu exelençia, la cruz en tierra los sayones[119] te pusieron encima. E tú, rex mirabilis, Deus et homo, conpliste su mandami/ento [14r] sin ninguna porfía. Prestamente bolviste las espaldas a la cruz, ofreçiéndote por nos dirías:[120] "Pater, adiuva me; factus sum obediens usque ad morten propter[121] filios Adami." Abriste tus reales braços; estendiste tus sanctas manos a que las enclavasen. E luego en punto travaron de ti, redemptor mío, commo canes fanbrientos. Uno tomó tu mano diestra; enclavóla. Otro la siniestra, estirando con grand fuerça, desconcertaron tus braços e espaldas. Otros tomaron tus santísimos pies sin piadat;[122] tiraron fasta que desconjuntaron[123] tu[s] santíssimas piernas. E con tres fieros[124] duros e rezias martilladas traspasaron e plegaron tus manos e pies en la cruz a su voluntad. E fincada la cruz en tierra, fueste alçado en alto por que la gente vulgar conosciesen commo tus enemigos tomaron conplida vengança de ti. Glorificado e alabado seas tú, Señor mío, que[125] [14v] tanta inpotençia de ti mostraste, seiendo tú Dios omnipotente, en aquella ora con ardiente caridat. Tú, Señor, salvador mío, obispo consagrado en la ara de la cruz, con soberana paciencia, tu boca apretada, cordero omilde, fueste sacrificado por nos commo omne verdadero. Llagado, quebrantado, descoyuntado, enclavado, lloraste lágrimas con dolor de las graves llagas que padeçías, ca estavas plegado en el madero, estirado, desfalleçido de la substançia humana cumpliendo la profecía de David: "Fixerunt manus meas et pedes meos, dinumeraverunt omnia ossa mea."[126] E ansí martirizado, querellándote con grandes dolores, dixiste al Padre: "Deus mcus, Dcus meus, ul quid me derelequisti?"[127] Con fuerte aflicçión commo omne que padeçías tan fuertes e soberanos

---

[119] *sayones*: executioners who carried out sentences.
[120] *dirías*: *r* written over, possibly changed from *c*.
[121] *propter*: second *p* added above the line.
[122] *piadat*: ant. *piedad*.
[123] *desconjuntaron*: ant. *desjuntaron*.
[124] *fieros*: *hierros*.
[125] *que la gente . . . que* written below the letter block.
[126] Psalm 21:17-18.
[127] Matthew 27:46 and Mark 15:34.

dolores que non ay coraçón que pensarlos pueda, caso que[128] la divinidat te esforçava que de ti nunca se partió. Señor, pues por mí tu esclava te plogo ser mártir en la cruz sufriendo [15r] dolores exçedientes a todas las penas de los mártires, yo te adoro, Dios e omne, colgado penado en la cruz. E te suplico, por reverençia de los graves dolores que sufriste de los tres fieros, me des virtud que yo cunpla los tres votos que a ti prometí, commo los cunplió sancta Elena.[129]

Capítulo xxviij. Ihesu, miserere mei, por virtud del dolor que sufriste en las llagas de tus manos e pies, por el ronpimiento de la carne, cuero, venas, por el encogimiento de los nervios, por virtud de la sangre coriente, tú, fons pietatis, te plogo darla tan abondosa sin ninguna escaseza por mí, aunque una sola gota todo el mundo podía salvar. Señor, yo te suplico, por la excelencia de las çinco plagas[130] tuyas, me otorgues çinco virtudes a mí neçesarias, de las quales yo caresco, videliçet devoçión, [15v] conoscimiento de mis pecados, perfecta contriçión de ellos, verdadera confesión de lengua, conplida satisfaçión de obra fasta mi fin, commo María Gipciaca.[131]

Capítulo[132] xxix. Ihesu, miserere mei, por virtud de la desonrra e grandíssima pena que padesçiste quando tú, criador del mundo, en la cruz sostenido fueste en dos clavos, tu cuerpo despojado entre dos ladrones deputado.[133] Commo malfechor fueste escarneçido, blasfemado de los que dezían: "Va qui destruis templum Dei, si rex Isrrael est, desçendat nunc de cruce."[134] Señor, pues por mí tu esclava sofriste

---

[128] *caso que*: ant. *aunque.*

[129] St. Helena (c.250-330), mother of Constantine the Great, became a Christian in later life, showing great faith and zeal. She was known for her kindness and charitable acts and considered herself a servant of religious people. She is traditionally associated with the finding of the True Cross.

[130] *plagas*: *llagas.*

[131] *Gipciaca*: written in the margin toward the binding and difficult to read. St. Mary of Egypt, fifth-century penitent and ascetic who, after a sinful early life as an entertainer, spent over 40 years in the desert doing penance.

[132] *Capítulo*: + *treinta* with dots above it to indicate that it is to be omitted.

[133] *deputado*: i.e., *diputado*, ant. *destinado, señalado.*

[134] Matthew 27:40, 42 and Mark 15:29, 32.

tantos baldones, yo te suplico que ordenes mi lengua que a ti alabe e al próximo non ofenda, e la alinpies de toda mentira por que yo cunpla tu voluntad.

Capítulo xxx. Ihesu, parçe michi, por el enxenplo que nos diste rogando por los [16r] que te penaron quando dixiste: "Pater, ignoce illis quia nesciunt quid faciunt",[135] Señor, yo te suplico me des graçia que yo perdone de coraçón a todos los que me injuriaren, egualmente bivos e muertos perdonando. Revoco todo lo que en contrario pensare o dixere. E te suplico que tú los perdones ansí commo yo quiero ser perdonada de ti, que te ofendo gravemente por maliçia, ignorançia, flaqueza, inadvertençia, commo grande pecadora que yo so.[136]

Capítulo xxxi. Ihesu, miserere mei, por la misericordia que obraste perdonando al ladrón, diziéndole: "Hodie mecum eris in paradiso",[137] Señor, yo te suplico que ansí plega a tu clemençia perdonar a mí, que sabes que non te sé llamar nin conosçer con la fe que este ladrón te llamó. Pero tal qual yo soy, digna de muerte eternal, creo que [16v] la tu misericordia no es menor oy para mí que fue para él. Señor, miénbrate[138] que soy tu sierva señalada de la señal de tu cruz e confieso tu fe.

Capítulo xxxij. Ihesu, miserere mei, por el muy entrañable dolor que pasaste despidiéndote de la tu muy amada madre, la qual con angustia e pena acataste con gravísimo pesar que rasgó tus entrañas commo aquél que la mucho amavas, querellándote le mostraste las llagas que tenías en la vestidura que della tomaste, queriendo dezir: "Señora madre, acata qual está tu fijo que de Espíritu Santo concebiste, sin dolor virgen pariste. E tú sabes que sienpre te fui omilde e obediente. E agora vees tan grand lástima de mí sin lo mereçer. Yo te ruego que por mi amor te esfuerçes e ayas paciençia, que ya se açerca la ora en que tengo de espirar. Yo te encomiendo a mi Padre que [17r] te consuele fasta el

---

[135] Luke 23:34.

[136] *so*: *soy*.

[137] Luke 23:43.

[138] *miénbrate*: ant. *recuérdate*.

terçero día que estaré apartado de ti. Encomiéndote a sant Juan,[139] mi deziplo, tómale por fijo." E adversus ad dicipulum dixisti: "Ei, ecce mater tua."[140]

E la dolorosa tu madre, sus braços abiertos, su cuerpo encorvado, obedeçió tu mandamiento, su cabeça inclinada, santiguarte[141] ya con su mano, que responder non podía porque su lengua era privada. Su espíritu tenía amortiguado, su coraçón era fecho ovillo de dolores al pie de la cruz desque te vido desnudo enclavar e oyó las rezias martilladas que rasgavan tus manos e pies. Vido cómmo estava tu cuerpo colgado de dos clavos, la sangre corer de las llagas tanto abondosa, tu cuerpo e rostro tanto diforme que non ay seso humano que conoçerlo pueda, ansí mesmo commo eras escarneçido, blasfemado. E oyó el grant clamor con lágrimas que diste al [17v] Padre, diziendo que eras desanparado dél. Llena de dolores, te quiso fablar e allegarse a ti; non tovo fuerça nin sentido para lo conplir. Resçibía la sangre que de ti corría con grant reverencia. E acatando en ti con grandíssimo amor, su coraçón fue rasgado, traspasado con cuchillo agudo, su ánima ensangustiada en tanto grado que la Señora reçibió martirio de dolores, ca ella sintió los tormentos que tú reçebiste propiamente contigo, así commo una mesma carne. E los dolores suyos multiplicaron a ti dolores sobre dolores.

E posumus credere que sant Juan, tu amado diçípulo, que presente fue a todos los tormentos que reçebiste, sufrió tan grant pesar que perdería todos sus sentidos, mesaría sus cabellos, daría fuertes golpes en su rostro e pechos con espesos[142] gemidos, abondosas lágrimas, en [18r] tanto grado que aquel día fue mártir. La Madalena con sobrepujante amor, dos hermanas de la Gloriosa con debdo[143] natural, Marta obligada de benefiçios, todos con grandíssimo amor e dolor mesarían sus cabellos;

---

[139] *Juan*: a smudge obscures the first three letters. The same occurs in the first words of the next two lines: *adversus* and *mater*.

[140] John 19:27.

[141] *santiguarte ya*: although the context suggests a hypothetical meaning, conditional forms appear as one word in the text.

[142] *espesos*: i.e., *repetidos, frecuentes*.

[143] *debdo*: ant. *deudo*, "kinship."

rasgarían sus caras, braços, manos e pechos; con agudos gritos lloraron amargosamente la cruel e desonrrada muerte que padesçías, timientes que la Gloriosa daría su ánima ese mesmo día.

Señor, pues por mí tu esclava, que lo non meresco, te plogo tanto padesçer e que la madre tuya, Reyna del Çielo, ese mesmo día fue martirizada de soberano martirio, yo te suplico, por el clamor que diste al Padre e por el martirio que pasó la Virgen tu madre, te plega dármela por abogada en mi vida e muerte, sea presente interçesora mía.

[Capítulo] xxxiij. Ihesu, miserere mei, por la amar/gura [18v] que padesciste quando "Siçio"[144] con dolor dexiste,[145] fiel e vinagre mixto fue dado a ti, fons ortorum, puteus aquarum vivençium.[146] Señor, pues tan abondoso eres e por mí tu esclava te plogo aver sed, yo te suplico me des virtud de abstinençia e me apartes del pecado de la gula en que me yo disuelvo, e faz digno mi coraçón que sienta dolor de tu passión para contemplar, sentir, llorar los dolores que [pa]deciste[147] como sannt Francisco.[148]

[Capítulo xxxiiij]. Ihesu, parce michi, por virtud de las palabras que tú, Ihesu, vida perdurable, dixiste con presura[149] de la muerte a la ora de la nona: "In manus tuas, Domine, comendo spiritum meum."[150] En ese momento el tu santíssimo spíritu fue apartado del tu santísimo cuerpo. Yo creo verdaderamente que la tu divinidat sienpre estudo[151] contigo en la cruz e en el [19r] sepulcro e decendió a los infiernos con el spíritu. Señor, pues por mí tu esclava quisiste morir, seyendo Dios eterno, yo te adoro Dios bivo verdadero e te suplico por la ecelençia de

---

[144] *Siçio*: John 19:28.

[145] *dexiste*: uncertain reading.

[146] Song of Solomon 4:15.

[147] *que*: + two marginal notes. The first note is an illegible word ending in *s*. The second note is *[pa]deciste* in faint letters.

[148] St. Francis of Assisi (1182-1226), founder of the Franciscan Order (Friars Minor and Poor Clares), believed in the literal imitation of Jesus and received the stigmata.

[149] *presura*: *opresión, aprieto, congoja.*

[150] Luke 23:46.

[151] *estudo*: ant. *estuvo.*

los méritos que en treinta e tres años con la tu gloriosa umanidat[152] meresçiste, e por reverençia de la muerte que por mí padesçiste, te plega perdonarme todos los pecados que he fecho cont[r]a ti, contra mi ánima e contra mis próximos desde que yo sope pecar fasta el presente momento en que estó.[153] E por lo alcançar reverente[154] digo: Domine Ihesu Christe, Filii Dei unigeniti, pone passionen, crucem et mortem tuam inter iudicium tuum et animam meam, nunc et in ora mortis mee largiri digneris. Qui vivis, et.[155] Kyrie eleison. Kyrie eleison. Christe eleison. Domine, miserere. Christus Dominus factus est obediens usque ad morten. Qui passurus ad/venisti [19v] propter nos. **P.**[156] Christe eleison. ℣. Qui expanssis in cruce manibus traxisti omnia ad te secula. **P.** Christe eleison. ℣. Qui prophetice promisisti: Ero mores[157] tua, o mors. **P.** Christe eleison. Domine, miserere. Christus Dominus factus est obediens usque ad mortem et cetera. Kyrie eleison. Kyrie eleison. Kyrie eleison. Domine, miserere. Christus et cetera.[158] Credo in Deum Patrem, et cetera.[159]

Suplicación.[160] Señor muy excelente, que muriendo en la cruz fueste vençedor, yo te ofresco alabanças quantas puedo, ansí commo los espíritus angelicales te alabaron con gozo de nuestra redenpçión diziendo:

---

[152] *umanidat*: initial *h* added in the margin in a different hand.

[153] *estó*: *estoy*.

[154] *reverente*: an additional *r* added interlinear at the end of the word.

[155] As this collect is addressed to the Son, the complete conclusion is: *Qui vivis et regnas cum Deo Patre in unitate Spiritus Sancti, Deus, per omnia saecula saeculorum.*

[156] *P.*: It is likely that this symbol is a rubrical direction indicating a pause in the middle of a verse or a change in singers. An asterisk is commonly used in modern liturgical texts.

[157] *mores*: read *mors*.

[158] *et cetera*: + *[au]tem atque crucis* in the margin.

[159] *Kyrie on 19r . . . et cetera*: Solemn Preces at the end of Lauds on Holy Thursday. The Creed and the Our Father conclude the Office.

[160] *Suplica* lightly crossed out.

24

Gloria in exçelsis Deo, et in terra et cetera.[161] Benediçio et claritas, sapiençia et graçiarum accio, honor, virtus, et fortitudo Deo nostro in secula seculorum, amen.[162] Graçias agamus Domino Deo nostro. Dignum et iustum est, vere dignum et iustum est, equm[163] et salutare nos tibi semper et ubique gracias agere. Domine sante, Pater omnipotens, eterne [20r] Deus, per Christum Dominum nostrum.[164]

Suplicaçión. Señor, pues tanto amaste los pecadores que te plogo redemirlos en la cruz, yo, Costança, indigna esclava tuya, te adoro e bendigo con todo mi entendimiento, memoria e voluntad, con el coraçón con la lengua, con todas las potencias que me tú diste, te rindo, te do[165] infinitos loores e graçias por la muerte que por mí reçebiste. E te suplico, con la mayor humildat que puedo, tú reçibas mi ánima e mi cuerpo, lo qual te ofresco todo segunt que me lo tú diste para que cunplas en mí tu voluntad entera, ansí commo criador en su criatura, e me endereçes a tu serviçio por qualquiera carera de las que tú sabes que a mí es provechosa, aunque a mí sea áspera. Señor, non acates mi pereza e olvidança nin mi atrevimiento e descono/cimiento [20v] con que me arriedro de ti, non queriendo pensar nin conosçer tus beneficios e gracias que de contino me fáçes ansí como oveja enferma, ciega que anda perdida sin pastor, que eres tú, Ihesu, mi redenptor que sabes que por sobervia e vanidat mía he cometido muchos pecados mortales, he quebrantado tus mandamientos e nunca conplí los votos que prometí en perfecçió[n].[166] Pequé con los çinco sesos[167] corporales cometiendo con ellos maliçias, erores sin cuenta segunt es claro delante el tu acatamicnto.[168] E tú, Señor mío, vees que caigo muchas vezes grandes

---

[161] *Gloria . . . et cetera*: called the *hymnus angelicus*, as its opening words are those of the angels announcing Christ's birth (Luke 2:14).

[162] *Benediçio . . . amen*: Apocalypse 7:12.

[163] *equm*: *aequum*, additional *u* above the line.

[164] *Graçias . . . nostrum*: dialogue at the beginning of the Preface of the Mass.

[165] *do*: *doy*.

[166] *perfecçió[n]*: squeezed into the margin.

[167] *sesos*: ant. *sentidos*.

[168] *acatamiento*: ant. *en tu presencia, delante de tus ojos*.

caídas en lazos peligrosos, en el lago de la muerte por mi grave culpa, e dellos non me puedo levantar por mi inpotençia si la tu mano de misericordia non me levanta e detiene con cadena del tu amor que fuerçe la pereça e dureza mía. Señor, co/mmo [21r] doliente que está en peligro, suplico a tu clemençia que ablandes la dureza de mi coraçón[169] e lo endereçes a ti, e le fagas capaz de la tu graçia pues eres poderoso. Crea in me cor mundum et espiritum rectum innova in viçeribus meis.[170] En otra manera yo quedaré llagada e muerta. In Deo, Domine, reminiscere miseracionum tuarum.

E non olvides nin aborescas este gusano de vil materia que se te ofreçe e rinde por cativa, e se lança delante tus pies commo la Magdalena pidiéndote perdón e merçed. Domine, misere[re] michi pecatriçe; puesto que por mi defecto non lo pido con tanto arepentimiento e contriçión commo ella lo pidió, Señor, la mengua es mía. Tú propio eres aquel que la perdonaste. Caso que la mi mesquindat e çeguedat es grande, con grannd nesçesidat llamo a ti físsico[171] que te mienbres que por tu clemençia me crias/te [21v] a la tu imagen e traxiste, aleluia, ley de graçia, a bevir en estado de religión sin mis mereçimientos. E agora peresco llena de pecados con muchas torpes manzillas sin número. Señor, pues fueste omne e conoçes la flaqueza de nuestra enferma carne, non te maravilles de mi ligereza, ca tú sabes que soy conçebida, naçida e criada en pecado. La naturaleza mía es enclinada a pecar, menguada e falleçida[172] de todo bien. Pues, Señor, acata mis dolencias peligrosas, sáname, vey[173] la mi neçesidat e acóreme.[174] Non esperes a mi virtud e fuerça que es ninguna, e tú sabes que te non puedo servir sin ti. Verdaderamente creo: Quod si vis potes me sanare.[175] Señor, non te pido riquezas nin días de vida[176] nin otros bienes tenporales, salvo que

---

[169] coraçón in the margin.
[170] Psalm 50:12, sung each morning at Lauds.
[171] físsico: ant. médico.
[172] falleçida: ant. "lacking."
[173] vey: vee.
[174] acóreme: i.e., acórreme, socórreme.
[175] Quod . . . sanare: based on Matthew 8:2 and parallels.
[176] non te . . . vida: compare 1 Kings 3:11.

me perdones, commo a la Magdalena, por que yo non sea lançada entre los que non [22r] bendiçen el tu santo nonbre, que tal qual yo soy te deseo bendezir por sienpre doquier que mi ánima sea.

Capítulo xxxv. Ihesu, miserere mei, por la llaga que fue fecha en tu costado quando[177] tú, verdadero pelicano, consentiste[178] a Longinos que lo abriese con la lança, emanó sangre e agua,[179] Señor, yo te suplico me libres del pecado de vengança, por lo qual los judíos obraron en ti tan dura muerte. Reprehendiéndolos la iglesia en presona[180] tuya dize: "Popule[181] meus, quid feci tibi aut in quo te costristavi?[182] Responde michi. Quia eduxi te de terra Egipti, parasti crucem Salvatori tuo? Agios o Theos. Agios isquiros. Agios athanatos, eleyson ymas. Santus Deus. Sanctus fortis. Sanctus et inmortalis, miserere nobis. Quia eduxisti[183] per desertum quadraginta annis, et magna[184] cibavi te, et introduxi in [22v] terram satis optimam, parasti crucem Salvatori tuo? Agios. Sanctus. Quid ultra debui facere tibi, et non feci? Ego quidem

---

[177] *quando* to the end of folio 22r is very difficult to read.

[178] *consentiste*: from *consentir*, "to agree with the dictates or opinion of another."

[179] The pelican has been widely used as a Christological symbol due to the supposed method of feeding its young. The reddish color of the breast feathers and the tip of the beak led to the idea that it drew blood from its breast to feed the little birds. The pelican's action was an apt symbol for the saving power of the blood and water issuing from Christ's wounded side. The name Longinus, from the Greek for lance, has been associated with the centurion who proclaimed the divinity of Christ after the crucifixion (Matthew 27:54, Mark 15:39) and with the soldier who pierced Christ's side (John 19:34).

[180] *presona*: i.e., *persona*.

[181] *Popule . . . Santus* at the end of the chapter: the Reproaches or Improperia are part of the Good Friday liturgy occurring after the prayers and before the adoration of the Cross. The opening words from Micah 6:3-4 are followed by the *Trisagion* (the thrice-holy) in Greek and Latin, which is twice more repeated after the versicles *Quia eduxi* and *Quid ultra*.

[182] *costristavi*: read *contristavi*.

[183] *eduxisti*: + *te* interlinear in a different hand. Read *eduxi te*.

[184] *magna*: read *manna*.

plantavi te vineam meam especio[si]ssimam et tu facta es michi nimis amara, aceto namque mixto cum felle sitim meam potasti, et lançea perforasti lactus[185] Salvatori tuo? Agios. Santus." **Capítulo xxxvj**. Ihesu, miserere mei, por la soledat que la tu madre sintió quando te vido muerto, e queriéndote deçender de la cruz, non tenía quien la ayudase nin sepultura en que te pusiesse, tanto apurada fue tu pobreza. E commo la Gloriosa suplicase a Nuestro Señor que proveiese lo nescesario, luego vinieron Nicodemus e Josep; ofreciéronse a fazer su mandamiento e traxeron todas las cosas neçesarias. Ayudaron a sannt Juan a descolgar el tu sacratíssimo cuerpo; a la ora de las bísperas te pussieron [23r] en braços de la Virgen, tu madre. Ella con grannt reverençia te reçibió. Señor, pues por mí tu esclava te plogo que la Gloriosa este grand dolor passase, yo te adoro e bendigo en sus braços. Benedictus[186] es, Domine Deus patrum nostrorum, et laudabilis et gloriosus in secula. Et benedictum nomen glorie tue quod est sanctum et laudabile et gloriosum in secula. Benedictus es in templo sancto glorie tue. Et laudabilis. Benedictus es super tronum sanctum regni tui. Et laudabilis. Benedictus es[187] super sceptrum divinitatis tue et laudabilis.[188] Benedictus es quia ambulas super penas ventorum. Et laudabilis. Benedictus es qui sedes super cherubim, intueris abissos. Et laudabilis. Benedicant te omnes angeli et sancti tui. Laudabilem et gloriosum in secula. Gloria Patri. Laudabili et glorioso[189] in secula. Sicut erat. Et laus et honor et potestas et inperium. Benedictus es, Domine Deus patrum nostrorum. Et laudabilis.

[**Capítulo xxxvii**]. Ihesu, parçe michi, por virtud del servi/çio [23v] postrimero que la Virgen tu madre te fizo quando enbolvió la tu gloriosa cabeça con el sudario e ungió el tu gloriosíssimo cuerpo con preçioso

---

[185] *lactus*: read *latus*.

[186] *Benedictus . . . laudabilis* at the end of the chapter: an adaptation from the canticle of the Three Young Men, see Daniel 3:52-55. Used on Sunday at Lauds.

[187] *es* interlinear.

[188] *laudabilis* added in the margin.

[189] *glorioso*: final *u* corrected to *o* and suppression mark erased.

28

unguento e te enbolvió en una sávana, con grande amor e reverençia
besó la tu santíssima boca. E sannt Juan e las Marías con grant vasca[190]
besaron tus pies, despidiéndose de la tu presençia. E ayudáronlo a poner
en el sepulcro a la ora de las cunpletas, que se cunplieron tus trabajos e
folgaste en ti mesmo en paz. Señor, pues por mí tu esclava quesiste ser
sepultado en el sepulcro terenal[191] e ajeno, yo te adoro e te suplico que
ordenes mi muerte para ti. Benedicite omnia et cetera.

Capítulo xxx[v]iij. Ihesu, miserere mei, por virtud de la fe que la
Gloriosa tovo en tres días quel tu sancto cuerpo estovo en el sepulcro
esperando tu resurecçión e confortó los tus deciplos que estavan [24r]
tristes e temerosos. Señor, yo tu esclava te suplico que[192] por exelençia
de las entrañas de la Gloriosa me libres ab omni inquinamento pecati,
ignorancie, fragilitatis, et malicie quod est peccatum in Spiritum
Sanctum. E me des esperança en ti cunplida por que yo muera confesando tu fe, commo sannt Pedro mártir quando reçibió martirio.

Christus factus es pro nobis obediens usque ad mortem. P. Mortem
autem crucis.[193]

Oraçio. Respice quesumus, Domine, super hanc famulan[194] tuam,
pro qua Dominus noster Ihesus Christus non dubitabit[195] manibus tradi
nocençium et crucis subire tormentum.[196]

O cruz potentísima, yo te adoro porque fuiste digna de sofrir en ti
Nuestro Redenptor; bendicho seas tú, madero que fuiste pena del fijo de
Dios e estrumento[197] de nuestra redempçión. O gloriosa cruz, fazme
digna [24v] que conosca tu exelençia[198] e me deleite en te alabar commo

---

[190] *vasca*: *basca, angustia*, "sick feeling, nausea."
[191] *terenal*: additional *r* above the line.
[192] *que* lightly crossed out.
[193] *Christus . . . crucis*: written in the same hand but set off in a much smaller letter. Used as Compline antiphon for the *Triduum Sacrum*, i.e., Holy Thursday, Good Friday, and Holy Saturday.
[194] *famulan*: read *familiam.*
[195] *dubitabit*: read *dubitavit.*
[196] Collect used for the Offices of the Triduum.
[197] *estrumento*: ant. *instrumento.*
[198] *exelençia*: *c* added above *xe.*

sannt Andrés,[199] por que seas sienpre en mi guarda, e tú me libres de mis enemigos vesibles e invesibles e de todas sus falsas ymaginaçiones, arterías, sotilezas, asechanças engañosas e lazos mortales. O cruz santa, por ti pido merçed a Aquel que en ti fue crucificado que te me dé a la ora de mi muerte por escudo entre mí e mis enemigos quando afincadamente acusarán mis culpas e querrán rebatar[200] mi ánima por me levar consigo adonde non ay redenpçión. Cruz virtuossa, por el vençimiento que Dios en ti fizo, libra mi ánima del su poder. Salve, cruz preçiosa que in corpore Christi dedicata es[201] et ex menbris eius tanquam margaritis ornata. Sucipe me pro amore illis[202] qui pependit in te magister meus Christus. O cruz inenarabilis. O cruz inextimabilis. O cruz la/udabilis [25r] que per totum mundum refulgens non me dimitas eramtem sicut ovem non abentem pastoren. O cruz fidelis, inter omnes arbor una nobilis, nulla silva talem profert fronde, flore, germine: dulce lignum, dulces clavos, dulce pondus sustinens.[203]

Hymno[204]

Vexilla Regis prodeunt,
fulget crucis misterium,
quo carne carnis Conditor
suspensus es patibulo.

---

[199] St. Andrew, apostle and brother of Simon Peter, celebrated on 30 November. According to tradition, he preached in Greece and Scythia and was crucified at Patras c. 70. Known for praising the mystery of the cross, Andrew is said to have hung on the cross alive for two days preaching the faith of Christ. He is often represented with an X-shaped cross in iconography.

[200] *rebatar*: ant. *arrebatar*.

[201] *es* interlinear.

[202] *illis*: read *illi*.

[203] *cruz fidelis . . . sustinens*: stanza 3 of the hymn *Lustris sex qui jam . . .* used on 14 September, the Exaltation of the Holy Cross, and at Lauds during Lent.

[204] Lenten hymn for Vespers, used as a processional hymn on Good Friday.

30

Quo vulneratus insuper
mucrone dire[205] lancee,
ut nos lavaret crimine,
manavit unda sangine.

Impleta sunt que concinit
David fidelis[206] carmine
dicendo nacionibus
regnavit a ligno Deus.

Arbor decora fulgida,
hornata Regis purpura,
electa digno stipite
tam sancta menbra tangere.

Beata, cuius brachiis
secli pependit precium,
statera facta corporis,
predanque tulit tartaris.

O crux, ave, spes unica,
hoc passionis tempore
auge piis iuticiam,[207]
reisque [25v] dona veniam.

Te, suma Deus Trinitas,
collaudet omnis spiritus,
quos per crucis misterium
salva, rege per secula, amen.

Antiphana. Super omnia ligna cedrorum tu sola excelsior in qua vita mundi pependit, in qua Christus trihunphavit, et mors mortem superavit in eternum[208] per signum crucis.

Oraçión. Omnipotens senpiterne Deus, qui humano generi ad inmitandum humilitatis exenplum salvatoren nostrum carnen sumere et cruçen[209] subire fecisti, concede propiçius ut et paciencie ipsius habere documenta et resurectionis consorcia mereamur.   Per eumdem.[210]

Capítulo xxxix. Ihesu, miserere mei, por la poderosa obra que tú feciste quando tu ánima decendió a los infiernos e por tu palabra quebranteste[711] las puertas, visitaste los santos padres e los alegraste con tu presençia e los sacaste [26r] de las tinieblas en que estavan.   Señor, yo tu esclava te suplico que por la tu virtud e amor de la Gloriosa libres

---

[205] *dire*: read *diro*.

[206] *fidelis*: read *fideli*.

[207] *iuticiam*: read *iusticiam*.

[208] Benedictus antiphon at Lauds on 14 September, the Exaltation of the Holy Cross.

[209] *carnen, cruçen*: last letter changed to *m*.

[210] Collect for Palm Sunday.

[211] *quebranteste*: read *quebrantaste*.

mi ánima que non sea lançada en el profundo lago del infierno, caso que lo yo meresco muchas vezes.

Beneditus²¹² Dominus, Deus Isrrael, quia visitavit et fecit redempcionem plebi²¹³ sue.²¹⁴ **Canticum angelorum**. Te Deum laudamus, et cetera.²¹⁵

Señor, por esta misericordia que tú feciste a los que estavan en el linbo te suplico que ayas merçed de todas las ánimas que están en purgatorio, principalmente las de mi padre e madre, e del señor rey don Pedro, e de la señora reyna doña Catalina,²¹⁶ e de mi señora doña María,²¹⁷ e de todos los que yo cargo tengo, todas las á[ni]mas que penan.²¹⁸ E te plega por reverencia de tu passión sacarlos de las penas que padeçen e levarlos a la tu gloria.

Capítulo quarenta. [26v] Ihesu, parce michi, por la tu resureççión quando poderosamente en tu propia virtud, así como león fuerte saliente del sepulcro, resurgente glorioso sol justicie,²¹⁹ te plogo apareçer e consolar a la Gloriosa madre tuya que deseando tu vista dezía: "Esurge gloria mea; esurge psalterium et citara." Tú enim dixisti: "Esurgam²²⁰ diluculo."²²¹ E tú, Señor, apareçístele con grannt resplandor, el pendón del tu vençimiento en la tu diestra, dixiste: "Dios te salve, reina del çielo, alégrate que yo vençí en la cruz e libré los pecadores del poderío

---

²¹² *Beneditus*: *c* added interlinear over *it*.

²¹³ *plebi*: read *plebis*.

²¹⁴ Canticle of Zechariah, Luke 1:68. The opening of the Gospel canticle sung every day at the end of Lauds.

²¹⁵ *Te Deum*: also called the Ambrosian hymn, sung at the end of Matins on Sundays and on major feast days.

²¹⁶ *Catalina*: + *e del rey do[n]* in the margin. Refers to Catherine of Lancaster, wife of Enrique III and granddaughter of Pedro I.

²¹⁷ María de Aragon, first wife of Juan II.

²¹⁸ *todas . . . penan* added at the end of the line, into the margin, and at the beginning of the next line in darker ink but the same hand.

²¹⁹ *justicie* + *E*.

²²⁰ *Esurgam*: final *t* corrected to *m*.

²²¹ *Esurge . . . diluculo*: Psalm 56:9.

de Satanás. Ya reçuçité, tú bivrás[222] comigo en gloria para sienpre. Muy cara madre, acata e ver aquí los sanctos padres que te bendizen e rinden graçias, porque en la carne que de ti tomé los redemí." La Virgen con alegría e reverençia te adoró diziendo: "Gloria tibi, [27r] Domine, qui surexisti a mortuis, Deus meus es tu et confitebor tibi, Deus meus es tu et adorabo te, quia convertisti plantum michi in gaudium michi et circundisti me leticia.[223] Hic est dies quam fecit Dominus, exultemos et letemur in ea".[224]

Señor, yo te suplico, por el gozo que diste a la Gloriosa con tu presencia, me da gra[cia], yo la si[ga], bendi[ga] e ala[be] con dilig[en]cia.[225] Christus resurgens ex mortuis iam non moritur, mors illi ultra non dominabitur quod enim[226] vivit Deo.[227] 𝖵. Dicite in nacionibus. P. Quia Dominus regnavit a ligno. **Oración.** Deus qui odierna[228] die per Unigenitum tuum eternitatis nobis aditum devita[229] morte reserasti, vota mea que perveniendo aspiras ecciam ajuvando[230] prosequere. Per eumdem. **Antiphana.** Regina celi, letare, alleluia. Quia quem meruisti portare, alleluia. Resurexit sicut dixit,[231] alleluia. Ora pro nobis [27v] rogamus, alleluia. 𝖵. Ora pro nobis, sancta Dei genitrix. P. Ut digni. **Oración.** Oremus. Graciam tuam quesumus, Domine, mentibus nostris infunde, ut qui, angelo nunciante, Christi Filii tui incarnacionem cognovimus, per passionem eius et crucem ad resurectionis gloriam perducamur. Per eumdem.

---

[222] *bivrás*: *vivirás*.

[223] *convertisti . . . leticia*: Psalm 29:12.

[224] *Hic . . . ea*: Psalm 117:24, used at the Easter Vigil.

[225] *yo te . . . me* written over a previous erasure, the remainder of the line and half of the following one filled with a decorative rectangle; *da . . . diligencia* added in the margin; *da*: read *dé*.

[226] *enim*: + *vivit* in the margin.

[227] Romans 6:9-10. These lines, plus the Latin section that follows, are used at Vespers on Easter Sunday.

[228] *odierna*: initial *h* added in a different hand.

[229] *devita*: *c* added above *it*.

[230] *ajuvando*: read *adjuvando*.

[231] *dixit*: *t* added interlinear.

Señor, pídote por merçed que ansí consueles e anpares las personas todas que están en tribulaçión. En espeçial a los que yo cargo e amor tengo. Dales graçia que bivan e mueram en verdadera penitencia. E en espeçial te suplico por nuestro señor el rey don Enrique,[232] que lo fortifiçes en virtudes e acrecientes su vida e le libres de tración[233] e ençalçes su corona.

Capítulo xlj. Ihesu, miserere mei, por el gozo que las Marías ovieron con [28r] la vista del ángel, certificadas de la tu resurecçión, e Santiago el menor quando te vido resucitado, e la Magdalena quando le tú apareciste en el huerto e nonbraste: "María." E ella con alegría te respondió: "Maestro, Señor",[234] conosciendo que tú eras aquel que la avías perdonado sus pecados e la conpliste de graçia. E con gozo dezía a tus deciplos: "Resurexit Christus spes mea, preçedet vos in Galilea."[235]

Capítulo xlij. Ihesu, miserere mei, commo perdonaste a sannt Pedro e le consolaste con tu presençia que estava triste llorando su pecado, Señor, yo tu esclava te suplico que me des graçia que ansí llore amargosamente todos mis pecados commo él. E pídote por merced que quites de mi coraçón todas dubdas contra tu [28v] fe e malos pensamientos, segunt tiraste la dubda a santo Tomás quando puso sus dedos en tus llagas e fue confirmado en la fe. E, Señor, alegra mi coraçón en tus obras, commo tus deçípulos fueron alegres de la tu resurecçión.

Capítulo xliij. Ihesu, miserere mei, por virtud de la solepnidat[236] que feçiste, conplidos los quarenta días de la tu resurecçión, dispidiéndote de la Virgen e de tus diziplos: gloriosa e poderosamente la tu sanctíssima humanidat con la virtuosa divinidat subiste a los çielos.

---

[232] Enrique IV. The name is abbreviated to include only the first five letters, which are somewhat squeezed together. It is written in darker ink than the surrounding words, indicating the possibility of a substitution for another name.

[233] *tración*: read *traición*.

[234] See Matthew 28:1-8, John 20:11-18, 1 Corinthians 15:7.

[235] Adaptation of the responsory at Matins on Monday and Thursday of Easter week. Similar to Matthew 28:7 and Mark 16:7.

[236] *solepnidat*: ant. *solemnidad*, "solemn ceremony."

En tu infinita virtud te absentaste[237] a la diestra de Dios Padre con Dios
Spíritu Sancto, tres personas un solo Dios que yo creo, adoro e
confiesso. E espero quel día del juizio as de venir juzgar los bivos e los
muertos, Dios et omne. Señor, yo tu esclava te suplico quel día de mi
muerte me judgues[238] [29r] segunt el que tú eres e tu propia condición,
non segunt mis obras, por virtud de tus amorosas entrañas. E por los
mereçimientos de la Virgen non te mienbres de las mis debdas.

Hympnum[239]

Eterne Rex altissime,
Redemptor et fidelium,
quo mors soluta deperit,
datur trihunphus gratie.

Tremunt videntes angeli,
versa vice mortalium:
culpat caro, purgat caro,
regnat Deus Dei caro.

Scandens tribunal dextere
Patris, potestas omnium
collata est Ihesu celitus,
que non erat humanitus;

Tu esto nostrum gaudium,
qui es futurus premium,
sit nostra in te gloria,
per cunta[242] semper secula.

Ut trina rerum machina
celestium, terestium[240]
et infernorum condita
flectat[241] genu iam subdita.

Gloria tibi, Domine,
qui escandis[243] supra sidera,
cum Patre, Sancto Spiritu,
in sempiterna secula. Amen.

[29v] **Antiphana.** O Rex glorie, Domine virtutum, qui trihunphator

---

[237] *absentaste*: corrected to *asentaste* by crossing out the *b*.

[238] *judgues*: ant. *juzgues*.

[239] Hymn used at Vespers and Matins of Ascension, followed by the
Magnificat antiphon, short responses, and prayer for the same feast.

[240] *terestium*: read *terrestrium*. See the same form in the fourth stanza of
the hymn on folio 32v.

[241] *flectat* has a suppression mark over the *a*.

[242] *cunta*: *cuncta*.

[243] *qui*: interlinear; *escandis*: *e* crossed out.

hodie super omnes celos acendisti, nec derelinquas nos orphanos, set micte[244] promissum Patris in nos Spiritum veritatis, alleluya. ℣. Elevata est magnificencia tua, alleluya. **P**. Super çelos, alleluya. **Oración**. Conçede quesumus, omnipotens Deus, ut qui hodierna die Unigenitum tuum redenptorem nostrum ad celos acendisse credimus, ipsi quoque mente in celestibus habitemus. Per eumdem[245] Dominum.

Capítulo quarenta e quatro. Ihesu, miserere mei, por la provechosa obra que tú feciste después de diez días de la tu asención, quando el tu Sancto Spíritu decendió con grant sonido en lenguas de fuego sobre la Gloriosa e apóstoles, los enflamó e confortó. Señor, yo tu esclava te suplico, Dios Spíritu Sancto que eres lux soberana, que alinpies mi entendimiento [30r] de la tiniebla en que estó e inflames mi coraçón de tu deseo. E me des contriçión, temor e tremor para te reçebir con aquella reverençia, humildat, linpieza que cunple[246] a mi salvaçión. Así mesmo te suplico que enbíes tu graçia sobre todas las dueñas deste monesterio e acreçientes sus virtudes e les des[247] buena fin, pues sabes tú el grant defecto mío commo soy nigligente en su regimiento, nin soy digna nin capaz para las castigar[248] por pobreza de sçiençia e juizio. Tú, Señor, cunpliendo lo que en mi fallesçe, te plega ordenar a ellas e a mí a tu serviçio.

Hympnum[249]

Veni, Creator Spiritus,
mentes tuorum visita,
inple superna gracia
que tu creasti pectora.

Qui Paraclitus diceris,
dopnum[250] Dei altissimi,
fons vivus, ignis, ca/ritas
[30v] et spiritalis uncio.

---

[244] *micte*: i.e, *mitte*.
[245] *eum*: repeated and crossed out.
[246] *cunple*: ant. *conviene*.
[247] *e les*: in darker ink + *des* in the margin.
[248] *castigar*: ant. *aconsejar, enseñar*.
[249] Hymn used at Terce of Pentecost and three days following.
[250] *dopnum*: *p* crossed out.

Tu septiformis gracie,
destre[251] Dei tu digitus,
tu rite promisum Patris,
sermone ditans gutur[a]:

Hostem repellas longius,
pacemque dones protinus,
ductore sit[253] te previo,
vitemus omne noxium.

Ascende[252] lumen sensibus,
infunde amorem cordibus,
infirma nostri corporis
virtute firmans perpeti.

Per te sciamus da Patrem,
nogscamus[254] atque Filium,
te utriusque Spiritum
credamus omni tenpore.

Sit laus Patri, cum Filio,
Sancto simul Paraclito,
nobisque mittat Filius
carissima[255] Santi Spiritus. Amen.

Prosa.[256] Veni, Sancte Spiritus, et emitte celitus luçis tue radium. Veni, Pater pauperum, veni, dator munerum, veni, lumen cordium. Consolator obtime,[257] dulcis ospes anime, dulce refrigerium. In labore requies, in extu[258] tenperies, in flectu[259] solacium. O lux [31r] beatisima, reple cordis intima tuorum fidelium; sine tuo numine nichil est in omine,[260] nichil est innoxium. Lava quod est sordidum, riga quod est aridum. Sana quod est saucium. Flecte quod est frigidum. Rege quod

---

[251] *destre*: i.e., *dexterae*.
[252] *Ascende*: i.e., *accende*.
[253] *sit*: read *sic*.
[254] *nogscamus*: i.e., *noscamus*.
[255] *carissima*: the hymnal reads *charisma*.
[256] This paragraph and the next as far as *P* are the sequence used at the gospel time on Pentecost Sunday.
[257] *obtime*: *optime*.
[258] *extu*: uncertain reading; should read *extremo*.
[259] *flectu*: i.e., *fletu*.
[260] *omine*: *h* written in at the beginning of the word.

est devium.[261] Da tuis fidelibus in te confidentibus sacrum septenarium. Da virtutis[262] meritum. Da salutis exitum. Da perenne[263] gaudium. Amen.

Antiphana. Veni, Sancte Spiritus, reple tuorum corda fidelium et tui amoris in eis ignem ascende, qui per diversitatem ligarum multarum gentes in unitatem fidei congregasti. ℣. Emitte Spiritum tuum et creabuntur. **P.** Et renovabis facien tere.[264]

Deus, qui corda fidelium Sancti Spiritus illustracione docuisti, da nobis in eodem Spiritu recta sapere[265] e de eius semper consolatione gaudere. Per eiusdem.

Yo, Costança, confiesso ser tanto grave peccadora, llena de gran/des [31v] peccados e sin ninguna virtud, que non soy digna de recebir [n]inguna gracia de las por mí suplicadas. Por tanto, con la humildat que puedo, suplico a todos los santos e santas nonbrados en esta oración que vos plega ofreçer vuestros trabajos e muertes por mí, suplicando a Nuestro Señor que por vuestros méritos le plega oír mis peticiones e faga comigo misericordia segunt su voluntad.

Este offiçio ordenó la mesma so[r]or sobre dicha.[266]

O Sapiencia, que ex ore Altissimi prodisti, atingens a fine usque ad finem, fortiter suaviterque disponens omnia: veni ad docendum nos viam prudencie. **Psalmus.** Laudate Dominum omnes gentes.[267]

---

[261] *est frigidum . . . devium*: the original text was erased and these words inserted in the space. The line should read: *Flecte quod est rigidum. Fove quod est frigidum.* Apparently *rigidum . . . est* was omitted in the process of correction.

[262] *virtutis*: *ti* written in above the line.

[263] *perenne*: *h* interlinear above the second *e*.

[264] *Antiphana. . . tere* in a smaller, very legible letter.

[265] *sapere* not very legible, as the ink seepage from the gold illuminated letter on 31v obscures some letters at the end.

[266] This Office marks a change from Easter to Advent, starting with the great "O" antiphon used at Vespers on 17 December and the following days until Christmas.

[267] Psalm 116 used at Vespers on Monday.

38

Antiphana. [32r] O Adonay, et dux domus Israel, qui Moysi in igne flamme rubi apparuisti et ei in Signai legem dedisti: veni ad redimendum nos in brachio extento. **Psalmus.** Ad te levavi.[268]

Antiphana. O Radix Iesse, qui stas in signum populorum, super quem continebunt reges os suum, quem gentes deprecabuntur: veni ad liberandum nos, iam noli tardare. **Psalmus.** Beati omnes qui.[269]

Antiphana. O Clavis David, et ceptrum domus Israel, qui aperis et nemo claudit, claudis et nemo aperit: veni et duc[270] vinctum de domo carceris, sedenten in tenebris et umbra mortis. **Psalmus.** De profundis cla[mavi].[271]

O Oriens, splendor lucis eterne et sol iusticie: veni et illumina sedentes in tenebris et unbra mortis. **Psalmus.** Domine non est exultatum.[272]

Capitula. Ecce virgo concipiet et pariet filium et vocabitur nomen eius Hemanuel; butirum et mel comedet ut[273] [32v] ciat[274] reprobare malum et eligere bonum.[275] **Responso.** Missus est angelus Gabriel ad Mariam virginem desponsatam Iosep, nuncians ei verbum; et expavecit virgo de lumine. Ne timeas, Maria, invenisti graciam apud Dominum; ecce conçipies, et paries Filium et vocabitur Altissimi Filius.[276] ℣. Dabit ei Dominus Deus sedem David, patris eius, et regnabit in domo Iacob in eternum. **P.** E vocabitur. Gloria. **P.** Altissimi Filius.

---

[268] Psalm 24 used at Prime on Sundays in Lent.

[269] Psalm 127 used at Vespers on Wednesday, as are the following two psalms.

[270] *duc*: read *educ*.

[271] Psalm 129.

[272] Psalm 130.

[273] *ut*: repeated at the beginning of 32v.

[274] *ciat*: i.e., *sciat*.

[275] Isaiah 7:14b-15, used at First Vespers on March 25, the Feast of the Annunciation.

[276] Responsory at Matins of Annunciation and first Sunday of Advent. Based on Luke 1:26-33, 35.

Hymno[277]

Conditor alme siderum,
eterna lux credencium,
Christe Rede[n]ptor omnium,
exaudi preces supplicum.

Qui condolens interitu[278]
mortis perire seculum,
salvasti mundum languidum,
donans reis remedium;

Vergente mundi vespere,
uti sponsus de talamo,
egressus bonestisima[279]
virginis matris clausula;

Cuius forti potençie,
genu flectuntur omnia,
celestia, terestia
nutu fatentur subdita;

Te deprecamur agie,
venture Judex seculi,
conserva nos in [33r] tempore
hostis a telo perfidi.

Laus, honor, virtus, gloria
Deo Patri et Filio,
Sancto simul Paraclito,
in sempiterna secula. Amen.

Verso. Rorate, celi, desuper et nubes pluant[280] iustum. ℞. Aperiatur terra et germinet Salvatorem. **Ad Magnificat**. O rex gencium et desideratus earum, lapisque angularis, qui facis utraque unum: veni, salva hominem quem de limo terre formasti. **Oraçión**. Excita quesumus, Domine, potenciam tuam et veni, ut ab iminentibus peccatorum nostrorum periculis te mereamur protegente[281] eripi, te liberante salvari. Qui vivis et regnas.

    Ad Conpletarium. Antiphana. O Hemanuel, rex et legifer noster, expectacio gencium et salvator earum, veni ad salvandum nos, Domine Deus noster. **Ad Nunc Dimitis. Antiphana**. Ave, gracia plena; Dominus tecum, benedicta in mulieribus et benedictus fructus ventris tui.

---

[277] Advent Vespers hymn, plus verse and response.

[278] *interitu*: final *m* erased.

[279] *bonestisima*: normally reads *honestisima*, but the initial *b* is clear in the codex.

[280] *pluant*: *t* blotted out.

[281] *protegente*: *gente* in a different hand.

40

Ad Matutinum. Antiphana. Ecce iam venit plenitudo temporis [33v] in quo misit Deus filium suum in uterum virginis Marie. Venite, adoremus.

Hymno[282]

Verbum supernum prodiens,
a Patre olim exiens,
qui natus orbi subvenis
cursu declivi temporis;

Illumina nunc pectora,
tuoque amore concrema;
audito ut preconio,
sint pulsa tamdem lubrica.

Iudexque cum post aderis,
rimari facta pectoris,
redens vicem pro abditis,
iustusque regnum pro bonis;

Non demum artemur malis
pro calitate criminis,
sed cum beatis conpotes,
simul perhennes celibes.

Gloria tibi Domine,
qui conceptus es in Maria virgine,
cum Patre et Sancto Spiritu.
in sempiterna secula. Amen

Este verso de suso que comiença: Gloria tibi Domine *diredes en fin de todos los himpnos, a todas las oras así del día commo de la noche, en su lugar.*
In Primo Noturno. Antiphana. Osecro, Domine, mite quis[283] missurus es, [34r] vide afliccionem populi tui, veni et libera nos, alleluya. **Psalmus.** Beatus vir.[284] **Antiphana.** Ecce in nubibus celi Dominus veni[285] cum potestate magna ad salvandum nos, alleluya. **Psalmus.** Domine, quid multiplicati.[286] **Antiphana.** Expectetur sicut

---

[282] Advent Matins hymn.
[283] *quis*: last two letters are very faint.
[284] Psalm 1. First psalm at Matins on Sunday.
[285] *veni*: + *et* added interlinear.
[286] Psalm 3. Third psalm at Matins on Sunday.

pluvia eloquium Domini et descendit[287] sicut ros super nos Dominus Deus noster, alleluya. **Psalmus**. Cum invocarem.[288] ℣. Ex Sion species decoris eius. ℟. Deus noster magnifeste[289] veniet. **Leccio prima**. Vidi portam in domo Domini clausam et dixit angelus ad me: "Porta hec quem vides clausa erit et non aperietur et vir non transibit per eam quoniam Dominus solus intrat et greditur per eam et erit clausa in eternum."[290] Set melior prophetie adimplecio. Quid est porta in domo Domini clausa nisi quod Maria semper erit intacta? Et quid est homo non transibit per eam ni quod Iosep non conosceret eam? Et quid est Dominus solus intrat et egredietur per eam ni quod Spiritus Sanctus inpregnabit [34v] eam et angelorum Dominus nascetur per eam? Et quid est clausa erit in eternum nisi quod Maria virgo est ante partum et virgo in partu et virgo post partum? **Responso**. Ecce ancilla Domini, fiat michi secundum verbum tuum[291] et inmediate Deus homo factus est in alvo virginis. **P**. Pro salute nostra. ℣. Pulcriores sunt occuli eius vino et dentes eius lacte candidiores. **P**. Pro salute. **Lectio secunda**. Dicat ergo Maria: "Porta facta sum celi. Ianua facta sum filio Dei, illa facta sum ianua clausa, per quem egressus pronus ad sui crucifixores; qui ad diçipulos suos clauso cenaculi ostio ut Deus ingressus est, homo ipse enim ad diçipulos per ostia ingressus est clausa; qui natus de ventre meo me matrem dimisit intactam, adimplevit ventrem meum divinitate et uterum meum non evacuavit castitate. [35r] Exivit ex ventre meo giganteo cursu magnificus et venter meus non est pudore vacuatus. Nec in conçeptione inventa sum sine pudore, nec in parturicione inventa sum cum dolore." **Responso**. Egredietur Dominus de Samaria ad portam que respicit ad orientem, et venit in Beleem ambulans super aquas redenpcionis Iudee. Tunc salus[292] erit omnis homo. **P**. Ora ecce veniet Deus noster. ℣. Et preparabitur in misericordia solium eius et sedebit

---

[287] *descendit*: *e* written above *i*.

[288] Psalm 4. Fourth psalm at Matins on Sunday.

[289] *magnifeste*: *manifeste*.

[290] *Porta . . . eternum*: based on Ezekiel 44:2; *greditur*: read *egredietur*.

[291] *Ecce . . . tuum*: Luke 1:38, used at Lauds of Annunciation.

[292] *salus*: another *u* added interlinear to convert *salus* to *salvus*.

42

super illud iudicans in equitate. **P.** Ora ecce.[293] **Leccio tercia.** O
Maria laudabilis, inter feminas eius ab angelo salutatur virginitas. Sola
inpregnata necque viciata, exhonerata nec vacuata, quia sic est ab angelo
salutata: "Ave, inquit, gracia plena, Dominus tecum; felix[294] umbilicus
castitatis que amplexus non tetigit maritalis." [35v] Considero
conceptum tuum, beata virgo, et espavesco, intueor partum tuum et
contremisco. Adoro filium tuum et revivisco. Enarra obsecro michi
quoniam meruisti dici mater Dei sponsaque filii Dei; quid quero indica
michi; set colloquenti tecum ignoce[295] michi quod audeam tibi loqui
servus, atque veniam ullus bonus et non inutilis et malus; ignosce michi
quod audeam cum sponsa Domini mei confabulari et tu indica michi
quomodo potuerit per te Dei filius generari. **Responsus.** Canite tuba in
Sion, vocate gentes, annunciate populis et dicite: Ecce Deus et homo
Salvator noster advenit.[296] *V̸.* Super que continebunt reges os suum,[297]
ipsum gentes deprecabuntur. **P.** Salvator. *V̸.* Gloria Patri. **P.**
Salvator.

    In ij° Noturno. Antiphana. Elevare, elevare, consurge,
Iherusalin;[298] solve vincla coli tui, captiva filia Sion, alleluya. **Psalmus.**
In Domino confido.[299] **Antiphana.** Consurge, [36r] consurge, induere
fortitudinem brachium Domini quia venit Salvator tuus, alleluya.
Psalmus. Domine, quis habitabit.[300] **Antiphana.** Ecce venit desideratus
cunctis gentibus et replebitur gloria domus Domini,[301] alleluya.
Psalmus. Dominus regit me.[302] Egredietur virga de radice Iesse. **R̸.**

---

[293] *Responso . . . ecce* used at Matins on the second Sunday of Advent.
[294] *felix*: uncertain reading of the first two letters.
[295] *ignoce*: i.e., *ignosce*.
[296] Response at Matins on the fourth Sunday in Advent.
[297] *Super . . . sum*: Isaiah 52:15.
[298] *Elevare . . . Iherusalin*: Isaiah 51:17.
[299] Psalm 10, used at Matins on Sunday, as are the following two psalms.
[300] Psalm 14.
[301] Haggai 2:8.
[302] Psalm 22.

Et flos de radice eis ascendet.[303] **Leccio iiii.** Audite, fratres, Mariam nobiscum colloquentem, carne absentem spiritu[304] presentem, verecundia virginali vultum avertentem a collocutore et indicantem quomodo inpregnata sit a Creatore. Eram, inquit Maria, in domo mea puella Iudea, ex femine David regis generata; adulta facta sum et desponsata coniugi et placui alteri non interveniente adulterio. Set intercedente Spiritu Sancto desponsata sum homini Iudeo et placui homini Deo. Desponsavit me vir Judeus.[305] Adamavit me Christus Deus. **Responsus.** Clama in fortitudine qui anuncias [36v] pacem in Iherusalim, dic civitatibus Iudee et habitatoribus Sion. **P.** Ecce Deus Salvator noster quem expectabamus advenit. ℣. Super montem excelsum ascende tu qui evangelizas Sion, exalta in fortitudine vocem tuam.[306] **P.** Ecce Deus Salvator. **Lectio v.** Ignoravit quidem Iosep sponsus meus quod me adamasset Deus meus et putavit quod[307] adulterio inpregnatus esset venter meus. Namque ignorante Iosep sponso meo, venit ad me quidam magnus Christi paraninphus: non patriarcha primus aut propheta egregius, set Gabriel arcangelus, facie rutilans, veste choruscans, incessu mirabilis, visitavit me, et perturbavit et salutavit, dixitque michi: Ave gratia plena, Dominus tecum. Dominus tecum inquid. Set plus quam mecum Dominus tecum. Set non sicut mecum. In me enim licet sicut[308] que Dominus memet ipsum creavit. [37r] Dominus patre autem nasciturus est Dominus. ℞. Montes Israel, ramos vestros expandite et florete et fructus facite. **P.** Prope est et iam veniet dies Domini. ℣. Rorate, celi, de super et nubes pluant iustum, apperiatur terra et germinet Salvatorem.[309] **P.** Prope est. **Leccio vi.** Ita Dominus est tecum ut sit in corde tuo et sit in utero tuo, adimpleat mentem tuam, adimpleat

---

[303] *Egredietur . . . ascendet*: Isaiah 11:1, short reading for Sext on Annunciation.

[304] *carne*: final *m* crossed out; *spiritu*: suppression mark over the *u*.

[305] *Judeus*: + *e* interlinear.

[306] Isaiah 40:9.

[307] *quod*: + *de* interlinear.

[308] *sicut*: + *sic* crossed out + *que* added below the line.

[309] *Rorate . . . Salvatorem*: from the Third Nocturn of Matins on Annunciation and Vespers of Sundays in Advent.

ventrem tuum, procedat formosus de utero tuo, tamquam sponsus de thalamo suo. Egrediatur rex ex intimo ventre tuo, tamquam sponsus de cubili suo, procedat princeps ex aula regali, ita ut virginitatem tuam non faciat violari. Dixitque illi: Quomodo fiet istud ut utero gravescam pudico, et inmunis sim a marito, quem penitus non cognosco, desponsata namque sum homini iusto? Set si illum non cognovero, unde erit quod generabo? Set si fieri potest [37v] ut concipiam intacta et generem clausa. Et³¹⁰ indica modum, et paratum invenies animum meum. Referit angelus modum conceptionis quod in verbo fieret Salvatoris. O, inquit, Maria. Spiritus Sanctus superveniet in te et virtus altissimi obumbrabit tibi.³¹¹ **Responsus.** Aspiciebam in visu noctis, et ecce in nubibus celi filius hominis venit,³¹² inductus carne nostre mortalitatis, et datum est ei regnum et honor. **P.** Et omnis populus, tribus³¹³ et lingue servient ei. ℣. Potestas eius, potestas eterna que non auferetur, et regnum eius, quod non corrumpetur. **P.** Et omnis.³¹⁴ Gloria Patri. **P.** Et omnis.

In iii⁰ Noturno. Antiphana. Anunciate populis et dicite: Salvator noster ec[c]e Deus venit, alleluya. **Psalmus.** Judica me Deus.³¹⁵ **Antiphana.** Ecce venit desideratus cunctis gentibus et replebitur gloria domus Dominum. **Psalmus.** Omnes gentes.³¹⁶ **Antiphana.** Hora est iam nos de sompno surgere³¹⁷ et aperti sunt occli nostri, surgere ad Christum quia lux vera est fulgens in mundo. **Psalmus.** Deus, [38r] in adiutorium.³¹⁸ ℞. Egredietur Dominus de loco sancto suo. ℣. Veniet ut salum³¹⁹ faciat populum suum. **Secundum Lucham:** In illo tempore, missus est angelus Gabriel a Deo in civitatem Gallilee cui nomen

---

³¹⁰ *Et* lightly crossed out.

³¹¹ *Spiritus . . . tibi*: Luke 1:35.

³¹² *Aspiciebam . . . venit*: Daniel 7:13.

³¹³ *tribus*: *tribubus* in the text with first *bu* crossed out.

³¹⁴ *Aspiciebam . . . venit* (*veniebat* in the Breviarium), *et datum . . . omnis*: used at Matins on the first Monday in Advent. *omnis*: *s* crossed out.

³¹⁵ Psalm 42, Matins on Tuesday.

³¹⁶ Psalm 46, Matins on Tuesday.

³¹⁷ *Hora . . . surgere*: Romans 13:11.

³¹⁸ Psalm 69, Matins on Thursday.

³¹⁹ *salum*: read *salvum*.

Nazareth, ad virginem desponsatam viro cui nomen erat Ioseph de domo
Davit, et nomen virginis Maria. Et reliqua.[320] **Omelia venerabile beati
Bede.**[321] Exordium redenptionis nostre, fratres Jerusalim, hodierna nobis
sancti evangelii lectio comendat. Que angelum de celis a Deo missum
narrat ad virginem ut novam in carne nativitatem filii Dei predicaret, per
quam nos, abiecta vetustate, noxia renovare atque inter filios Dei
conputari possimus. Tu autem, Domine. **Responsus.** Ecce iam venit
plenitudo temporis in quo misit Deus filium suum in terris, in utero
virginis Marie, factum sub lege. **P.** Ut eos qui in lege erant redimeret.[322]
℣. Prop/ter [38v] nimiam caritatem suam qua dilexit nos, Deus filium
suum misit in similitudinem carnis peccati.[323] **P.** Et eos. **Lecio viiiº.**
Ut ergo ad promisse salutis mereamur dona pertingere, primordium eius
intenta curemus aure percipere. Missus est, inquit, angelus Gabriel a
Deo in civitatem Galilee cui nomen Nazareth, ad virginem desponsatam
viro cui nomen erat Iosep. **Responsus.** Intuemini quantus sit iste
gloriosus qui ingreditur ad salvandas gentes, ipse est Rex iusticie. **P.**
Cuius generaçio non habet finem. ℣. Precussor pro nobis ingreditur,
secundum ordinem Melchissedec pontifex factus est in eternum.[324] **P.**
Cuius. **Lectio novena.** Aptum profecto humane restauracionis
principium ut angelus a Deo miteretur ad virginem partu consecrandam
divino. Quia [39r] perdicionis prima humane fuit causa cum serpens a
diabolo mitebatur ad mulierem spiritu superbie decipiendam: ymo ipse
in serpente diabolus veniebat, qui genus humanum deceptis parentibus[325]

---

[320] *missus . . . Maria*: Luke 1:26-27. *Et reliqua* indicates that this is just
the beginning of the reading which would extend to verse 38. Read at Matins
on 8 December, the Feast of the Immaculate Conception.
[321] St. Bede the Venerable, confessor and doctor of the Church, devoted
himself to study and especially to explanation of the Scriptures. *Exordium . . .
possimus* plus *Lectio viiiº* and *Lectio novena* are from the beginning of Bede's
Homily 3 for Advent.
[322] *venit . . . redimeret*: Galatians 4:4-5.
[323] *Ecce . . . peccati*: at Matins in Advent. The responses and antiphons
in the remainder of this office are from the Advent liturgy.
[324] *Precussor* (i.e., *precursor*) . . . *eternum*: Hebrews 6:20.
[325] *parentibus*: original *pe* changed to *pa*.

primis inmortalitatis gloria nudaret. **Responsus.** Aspiciens a longe, ecce video Dei potenciam venientem et nebulam totam terram tegentem. **P.** Ite oviam[326] ei et dicite. **P.** Nuncia nobis, si tu es ipse qui regnaturus es in populo Israel. ℣. Quique terrigine et filii hominum simul in unum dives et pauper. **P.** Ite ecita, Domine, potenciam tuam et veni ut salvos facias nos, que propter clemenciam tuam frater noster fieri dignatus es carnem nostram assumendo. **P.** Nuncia nobis. ℣. Ostende nobis, Domine, faciem tuam et salvos fac nos. **P.** Qui regnaturus. ℣. Gloria. **P.** In populo.

In Laudibus. ℣. Verbum caro factum est, alleluya. **P.** In virgine Maria. **In Laudibus. Antiphana.** In illa die stillabunt montes [39v] dulcedinem, et colles fluent lac et mel, alleluya.[327] **Antiphana.** Urbs fortitudinis nostre Sion, Salvator ponetur in ea murus et antemurale. Aperite portas que nobiscum Deus. **Antiphana.** Jocundare, filia Sion, exulta satis, filia Iherusalim. Ecce Dominus venit ad salvandum nos, alleluya. **Antiphana.** Dominus veniet, occurite illi dicentes: Magnum principium et regni eius non erit finis. Deus fortis dominator, princeps pacis, alleluya. **Ps.** Benedicite.[328] **Antiphana.** Qui venturus est ven[329] Deus homo et iam non erit timor in finibus nostris, alleluya. **Psalmus David.** Laudate Dominum.[330] **Capitula.** Ecce dies veniunt, dicit Dominus, et suscitabo Davit germen iustum et regnabit rex et sapiens erit et faciet iudicium et iusticiam in terra.[331]

Hymnus[332]

Vox clara ecce intonat,
obscura quaeque increpat.
Pellantur eminus sonpnia,
ab ethere Christus promicat.

Mens iam resurgat torpida,
que sorde extat saucia;
sidus re/fulget [40r] iam novum,
ut tollat omne noxium

---

[326] *oviam*: *obviam*.
[327] *In . . . mel*: Joel 3:18; *montes*: repeated on 39v.
[328] Daniel 3:57-88.
[329] *ven*: + *t*, correcting *ven* to *venit*.
[330] Psalm 148.
[331] Jeremiah 23:5.
[332] Advent hymn at Lauds.

Ex sursum Agnus mittitur,   Secundo ut cum fulserit,
laxare gratis debitum;   mundu[m]que horror cinxerit;
omnes pro indulgencia   non pro reatu puniat,
vocen demus cum lacrimis.   set pius tunc nos protegat.

Gloria tibi, Domine.

℣. Constantes estote, alleluya. ℞. Quia mulier circundat virum,
alleluya. **Ad Benedictus. Antiphana.** Quomodo fiet istud, angele Dei,
que virum non conosco? Audi, Maria virgo Christi: Spiritus Sanctus
superveniet in te, et virtus Altissimi obumbrabit tibi, alleluya.
Canticum. Benedictus Dominus. **Oración.** Deus qui de beate Marie.[333]
Esta oración se diga a todas las oras. **Antiphana.** In illa die.
Ad Prima. Capitula. Regi seculorum.[334] ℞. Ihesu Christe, Filii
Dei vivi, miserere nobis, alleluya, alleluya. ℣. Qui venturus es in
mundum propter nos. **P.** Alleluya, alleluya. Gloria Patri. **P.** Ihesu
Christe. Exurge Domine.
Ad iiiª. Antiphana. Orbis fortitudinis nostre Sion, Salvator.
Capitula. Ecce dies [40v] veniunt. ℞. Verbum caro factum est,
alleluya, alleluya. ℣. In virgine Maria, alleluya. **P.** Gloria Patri. ℣.
Verbum. ℞. Veni ad liberandum. ℣. Ostende faciem tuam et salvi
erimus.
Ad viª. Antiphana. Iocundare. **Capitula.** In diebus illis salvabitur
Iuda et Israhel habitabit confidenter, et hoc est nomen quod vocabunt
eum: Dominus iustus noster.[335] ℞. Veni ad liberandum nos. Domine
Deus virtutum. ℣. Ostende facien tuam et salvi erimus. **P.** Alleluya,
alleluya. ℣. Ostende nobis, Domine, misericordiam tuam. **P.** Et
salutare tuum da nobis. ℣. Qui venturus.
Ad ixª. Capitula. Erit in novissimis diebus preparatus mons domus
Domini in vertice moncium, et levabitur super colles et fluent ad eum

---

[333] The full text of this prayer is given on 41v-42r. Used at Lauds on 11
October, the Feast of the Motherhood of the Blessed Virgin Mary.
[334] 1 Timothy 1:17, the little chapter at Prime.
[335] Jeremiah 23:6.

48

omnis gentes.[336] [℟.] Ostende nobis Domine misericordiam tuam, alleluya. ℣. E salutare tuum da nobis. **P.** Alleluya, alleluya. Gloria Patri. ℣. Constantes estote, alleluya. **P.** Quia mulier circundat virum, alleluya. [41r]

Ad Vesperas. Super psalmus antiphana.[337] [S]piritus Sanctus in te descendet, Maria, ne timeas, habebis in utero filium Dei, alleluya. **Psalmus.** Dixit Dominus.[338] **Antiphana.** Leva, Iherusalim, occulos tuos et vide potenciam Regis. Ecce Salvator venit tibi solvere te a vinculo, alleluya. **Psalmus.** Confitebor.[339] **Antiphana.** Erunpant montes iocunditatem et colles iusticiam que lux mundi Dominus in potestate venit, alleluya. **Psalmus.** Beatus vir.[340] **Antiphana.** Ecce venit Deus et homo de domo David sedere in trono, alleluya. **Psalmus.** Laudate, pueri.[341] **Antiphana.** Iam venit dominator Dominus et nomen eius Hemanuel vocabitur, alleluya. **Psalmus.** Laudate Dominum.[342] **Capitula.** Ecce dies veniunt dicit. **Hymnus.** Conditor alme *ut supra.* ℣. Verbum caro factum est, alleluya. **P.** In virgine Maria, alleluya. **Ad Magnificat. Antiphana.** Hec dies quam fecit Dominus, hodie Dominus aflictionem populi sui respexit et redempcionem misit, hodie mortem quam femina intulit, femina fugavit. Hodie Deus homo factus est, id quod fuit remansit et quod non erat asumpsit. [41v] Ergo exordium nostre redemptionis devote recolamus et exultemos dicentes: Gloria tibi, Domine, alleluya.

Ad Conplectorum. Super salmus antiphana. Ecce venit Dominus protector noster, sanctus Israel, coronam regni Ihesus[343] in capite suo, alleluya. **Ad Nunc Dimictis. Antiphana.** Salvator noster venit, Dominus Ihesus Christus, que reformabit corpus humilitatis noster, configuratur corpori claritatis sue, alleluya.

---

[336] Isaiah 2:2.
[337] There is a 3-4 letter blank space after *antiphana*.
[338] Psalm 109.
[339] Psalm 110.
[340] Psalm 111.
[341] Psalm 112.
[342] Psalm 116.
[343] *Ihesus* in a different hand.

INCIPIT OFICIUM INCARNACIONIS DOMINI NOSTRI
IHESUS CHRISTI

Oficium. Intuemini quantus sit iste gloriosus qui ingreditur ad salvandas gentes, ipse est Rex iusticie. Cuius generacio non habet finem. ℣. Propter nimiam caritatem suam qua dilexit nos,[344] Deus filium suum misit in mundum.

Oracio. Deus, qui de beate Marie virginis utero verbum tuum angelo numciante carnem suscipere volvisti, presta supplicibus tuis, ut [42r] qui vere eam genitricem Dei credimus, eius apud te intercessionibus adiuvemur. Per eumdem.

Lectio Libri Sapientie. Dilectus meus descendit in ortum suum ad areolam aromatis ut pascatur montes[345] et colligat lilia. Ego dilecto meo et dilectus meus michi qui pascitur inter lilia.[346] Dilectus meus candidus et rubicundus, electus ex millibus. Capud eius aurum optimum, come eius quasi elate palmarum. Occuli eius sicut columbe super rivulos aquarum que lacte sunt lote et resident iuxta fluenta plenissima. Gene illius sicut areole aromatum consite a pimentariis.[347] Labia illius lilia distilancia et mirram[348] primam. Manus eius tornatiles auree, plene iacintus. Venter eius eburneus distintus saphiris. Crura illius colupne marmoree, que fundate sunt [42v] super basses argenteas. Species eius ut Libani, electus ut cedri. Gutur eius suavissimum et totus desiderabilis. Talis est dilectus meus et iste est amicus meus, filie Iherusalim.

Responsus. Dominus dixit ad me: Filius meus es tu, ego hodie genui te.[349] ℣. Constantes estote et letamini quia mulier circundat virum, hec est virgo Maria puela intacta, alleluya. ℣. Rex pacificus

---

[344] *Propter . . . nos*: Ephesians 2:4.

[345] *montes*: the Vulgate reads *in hortis*.

[346] *Dilectus . . . lilia*: Song of Solomon 6:1-2. The rest of the reading is from 5:10-16.

[347] *pimentariis*: *pigmentariis*.

[348] *mirram*: read *myrrham*.

[349] Psalm 2:7 and repeated in Acts 13:33 *et alibi*.

incarnatus est hodie in uterum virginis carnem nostram asumendo cuius vultum[350] desiderat universsa terra.

Secundum Lucham:[351] In illo tempore, missus est angelus Gabriel a Deo in civitatem Gallilee cui nomen Nazareth ad virginem disponsatam viro cui nomen erat Iosep de domo David et nomen virginis Maria et ingressus angelus ad eam dixit: "Ave, gracia plena, Dominus tecum, benedicta tu in mulieribus." Que cum audisset turbata est in sermone eius [43r] et cogitabat qualis esset ista salutacio. Et ait angelus ei: "Ne timeas, Maria, invenisti graciam apud Deum. Ecce concipies in utero et paries filium et vocabis[352] nomen eius Jhesum, hic erit magnus et Filius Altissimi vocabitur. Et dabit illi Dominus Deus sedem Davit patris eius et regnabit in domo Iacob in eternum et regni eius non erit finis." Dixit autem Maria ad angelum: "Quomodo fiet istud quoniam virum non cognosco?" Et respondens angelus dixit ei: "Spiritus Sanctus superveniet in te et virtus Altissimi obumbrabit tibi, ideoque et quot nascetur ex te sanctum vocabitur Filius Dei. Et ecce Helisabeth cognata tua et ipsa concepit filium in sanetute[353] sua. Et hic mensis est sextus illi que vocatur sterilis quia non erit imposibile apud Deum omne verbum." Dixit autem Maria ad angelum: "Ecce ancilla Domini, fiat michi secumdum verbum [43v] tuum."

Ofrenda. Descendit de celo Deus verus a patre genitus, introivit in uterum virginis moram faciens novem mensibus. Verus Deus et homo conditor mundi, alleluya. **Sacramenta.**[354] In mentibus nostris, Domine, vere fidei sacramenta confirma ut qui conceptum de virgine Deum verum et hominem confitemur, per eius salutifere resurreccionis potenciam, ad eternam mereamur pervenire leticiam. Per eumdem.

---

[350] *vultum*: *u* added interlinear correcting *ultum* to *vultum*.

[351] Luke 1:26-38. Generally used on the following feast days: 25 March, Annunciation; 8 December, Immaculate Conception; and 31 May, Blessed Virgin Mary, Queen.

[352] *vocabis*: corrected from *vocabitur*.

[353] *sanetute*: *c* added above the first *e*; read *senectute*.

[354] Used in votive masses of the Blessed Virgin Mary. The abbreviation *Sac̄* is written in the margin. In the structure of the Mass, a prayer called the Secret Prayer is recited silently by the priest after the offering.

51

Sanctus.[355] Sanctus. Sanctus. Dominus Deus sabbaoth. Pleni sunt celi et terra gloria tua, ossana in excelsis. Beneditus qui venit in nomine Domini, osana[356] in excelsis. Agnus Dei qui tollis peccata mundi, miserere nobis. Agnus Dei qui tollis peccata mundi, miserere nobis. Agnus Dei qui tollis peccata mundi, dona nobis pacem. **Comunicanda.** Ut [verbum] caro factum est pro nobis [44r] in uterum virginis gloriose.

Post comunicanda. Graciam tuam quesumus Domine mentibus nostris infunde; [ut qui] angelo nunciante Christi Filii tui incarnacionem cognovimus per passionem eius et crucem ad resurecionis gloriam perducamur. Per eumdem.

Estas oras que se siguen ordenó la dicha soror de la Orden de Sancto Domingo de los Predicadores.[357]

IN COMEMORACIONE CLAVORUM PASSIONIS CHRISTI

In primis Vesperis. Super psalmus antiphana. O fortissimi clavi, omnes vos benedicimus qui potentes fuistis rumpere manus et pedes agni inmaculati Christi crucifixi. **Psalmus.** Laudate *et cum reliquis.*[358] **Capitula.** O dilectissima brachia et crura regalia, que cum ferventissima caritate et fortitudine mirabili susti/nuistis [44v] per manus impiorum asperis funibus disconiungi. **Responsum.** Avete, precciosissime plage Christi Ihesu, fuistis enim in suo corpore formate pulchre, de suisque menbris rescepistis valorem preciosissimum super lapides preciosos. **P.** Omnes vos adoramus et bendicimus in.[359] V̌. Ille qui vos propter nos

---

[355] The *Sanctus* and the *Agnus Dei* were sung at every mass.
[356] *osana*: last letters of the word are faded away as is much of the next six lines up to the end of the folio.
[357] A cross is drawn in the margin beside these lines.
[358] This refers to Psalms 112, 116, 145, 146, 147 used at First Vespers of major feasts.
[359] *bendicimus in: benedicimus in eternum.*

52

recepit vestra nobis indulgeant virtute. **P.** Omnes vos adoramus.
Gloria Patri. **P.** Omnes.[360]

Hymnum

Eterne Rex Altissime,
Pater superne glorie,
qui redemptorem hominis
tuum dedisti Filium;

O amor admirabilis,
qui filium pro servulis
dedisti suis emulis
in cruce ad inmolandum:

Flammam acende[361] cordium
tui amoris intimi
in nobis tuis famulis
ne simus tibi ingrati.

Ihesu vere pelicane
qui mortuos quos[362] vidisti
filios ut ipsi viverent
tua viscera rupisti.

Vivificatos sanguine
vultu benigno respice,
ne pereant in prelio
tuo defende clipeo.

Gloria tibi, Domine,
qui per clavorum vulnera
tuum dedisti sanguinem
redenptionis precium.

[45r] ℣. O felicissimi clavi passionis Christi. ℟. Qui medicina vulnerum nostrorum fuistis. **Ad Magnificat. Antiphana.** Benedictam et honorantissimam te Domini matrem laudamus, quia ad pedem crucis pro peccatis nostris cor tuum atque menbra inflammasti visceraque tua fuerunt cremancia sic viva pruna, ac tota te transformasti in illas metiras plagas filii tui; quia ambor[363] caro est una.[364] **Oracio.** Omnipotens sempiterne Deus, respice humilium vota et presta ut per clavorum et vulnerum Filii tui Domini nostri Ihesu Christi comemoracionem quam

---

[360] *propter . . . Omnes:* inserted at the bottom of the page. Insert indicated by a red cross in the text after *vos* and in the margin.
[361] *acende:* another *c* added interlinear.
[362] *quos:* read *quum.*
[363] *ambor:* read *amborum.*
[364] *tua . . . una:* inserted at the bottom of the page.

devote celebramus, vulnerum peccatorum nostrorum medelam et animarum solamen consequi mereamur. Per eumdem.

Ad Conpletam. Crucifixus est Christus in cruce, ut inimicos suos redimeret et conciliaret Deo Patri. **Psalmus.** Cum invocare[365] *cum reliquis.*

Hymnum

Dulces clavi[366] amabiles
duri tamen et asperi,
Christo fecistis vulnera
manus figendo et pedes.

Ausi fuistis rumpere
illa menbra regalia
Christi vincentis impium
ator[367] eius imperium.

Ihesu Salvator seculi,
verbum [45v] Patris Altissimi,
tuorum clavorum memores
a fauce serva tartari

Gloria tibi, Domine,
qui per.[368]

Ad Nu[n]c Dimitis. Antiphana. Christus Dominus factus est obediens usque ad afixionem clavorum et dirum crucis patibulum.[369]

Invitate. Regem crucifixum adoremus, Dominum pro nobis in cruce tribus clavis confixum. **Psalmus.** Venite.[370]

Hypnum

Eterni Pater luminis,
plasmator alme hominis,
facturam tuam redimens
indulge nobis miseris.

O Fili, princeps inclite,
victor dueli Satane,
conserva tuos famulos
tuo redenptos sanguine.

---

[365] Psalm 4 used on Sunday at Compline.
[366] *clavi*: final *s* crossed out.
[367] *ator*: unclear reading.
[368] All the hymns in this Office will have the same final stanza as *Eterne rex* (p. 52).
[369] Adaptation of the Good Friday antiphon.
[370] Psalm 94 is used each day at Matins.

Pie redenptor humilis
nature lapse fragilis,
in huius vite fluctibus
esto nobis propicius.

Confringe clavis viscera
nostre carnis mortifera,
ut crucifixi in sua
consequamur celestia.

Gloria tibi Domine.

In primo Noturno. Super salmus antiphana. Ordinasti, Pater clementissime, inocentissimum filium tuum tradi in ma/nus [46r] nocencium pro redenptione nostra. **Psalmus.** Beatus vir qui non abiit.[371] **Antiphana.** O agnus innocens, Christe redenptor, qui tribus clavis confixus in cruce fuisti pro redemptione servorum tuorum. **Psalmus.** Domine, quid multiplicati sunt.[372] **Antiphana.** O piissima mater et virgo intacta, que confixa fuisti illis tribus clavis in quibus vidisti filium tuum suspensum. **Psalmus.** Cum invocarem. [℣.][373] Vulneratus est Christus propter iniquitates nostras. ℟. Et langores nostros ipse portavit.

Leccio prima. O bone Ihesu, quantis et quam inextimabilibus modis te totum dedisti nobis indignis servis tuis. Non enim sufecit illi tuo ardentissimo amori quem nobis ostendere venisti, te de celo in terram descendisse et tuam incomprehensibilem deitatem velamento nostre mortalis carnis operuisse, et sic te monstrasse occulis mortalium, nec sufecit quod tuum mundissimum et preciosissimum sanguinem ad abluendum nostrorum macu/las [46v] peccatorum, in tua tenerrima etate fundere cepisti. Verum voluisti nobis ostendere perfectissimum ipsius tui amoris gradum, quo nos inefabiliter diligere dignatus es quando non solum pro amicis, sed eciam pro inimicis tuis improperiosam passionem sustinuisti. Quisnamque posset a fletibus et lacrimis continere si mentalibus occlis atente et devote prospiceret quomodo tu, Domine, Rex celorum, mostrando te verum hominem, naturaliter timuisti paratam tibi

---

[371] Psalm 1 used at Sunday Matins.
[372] Psalm 4 used at Sunday Matins.
[373] The *Psalmus* indication for Psalm 4 is mistakenly inserted after the psalm and ℣ is omitted. For the versicle and response, cf. Isaiah 53:4, 5.

horribilem mortem? Et cum timore illius in orationem quam Patri humiliter fecisti, in tanta fuisti positus agonia, quod sudor tuus factus est sicut sudor sanguinis decurrentis in teram.[374] Set quamvis tua mundissima et delicatissima caro fuerit infirma, et illius sensualitas recusaverit pati, spiritus tamen tuus mansit victor et trihunphans. [47r] E sic cum Patris perfectissima obediencia et nostri mortalium suprema dilectione tu, eterna vita, te sponte morti obtulisti, voluntatem tuam voluntati Patris conformando. Et tunc invincibili cum fortitudine expetasti[375] inimicos tuos in orto.

O inestimabilis dilectio tue caritatis, dulcissime Ihesu, qui ut servum redimeres te ipsum tradidisti, nec timuisti gentiles armatos, nec Iudeos acusantes, nec iniuriantes ministros, nec horruisti ab eis ligari et duci ligatum coram sacerdotibus et preside Pilato qui[376] tuis tradidit emulis ad crucifigendum. Set quis, o amantissime Ihesu, a singultibus et suspiriis cessare deberet, cum eisdem occlis pie intueretur te, Dominum, Regem seculorum, iuvenem elegantem, florem tocius[377] carnis, non abentem[378] speciem nec decorem, baiulantem[379] in humero tuo versus mon/tem [47v] Calvarie ponderosum lignum crucis in quo mortem subires? Ecciam quomodo tu, bone Ihesu, quando ad locum horendum fatigatus et anxiatus, flagelatus et duris spinis coronatus accesisti, te spreto et abiecto, vestibus tuis spoliato, tuo preciosissimo corpore nudo et in spectaculum populi posito, te inimicis tuis obtulisti. Et sine perfidia aut resistencia aliqua extendisti tua brachia regalia, et tuas delicatas manus humiliter aperuisti, ac adaptasti sacratissimos pedes tuos ut inimici tui operarentur in te voluntatem suam. Et clauso ore atque constricto sustinuisti acerbissimas rupturas et vulnera crudelissima trium duris-simorum clavorum, qui cum inpetuosis maleorum ictibus accerrime

---

[374] *teram*: additional *r* added above the line converting *teram* to *terram*.

[375] *expectasti*: the first two letters and the first *t* are written over to create *expectasti*.

[376] *qui*: + ink blot that may cover one or two letters.

[377] *tocius*: i.e., *totius*.

[378] *abentem*: *h* added at the beginning of the word.

[379] *baiulantem*: an ink blot obscures the letters between *a* and *m*.

resecarunt et penetrarunt cutem et carnem, nervos et venas manuum et peduum tuorum.

Set nos mise/rabiles [48r] prevaricacionis filii, magna cum cecitate incognicionis, et in grandi contemptu et vanitate ingratitudinis, non cognoscimus ipsum tuum tan gratissimum amorem, nec sentimus tua innumerabilia beneficia, tam stupore quam admiracione plena, nam non cum atencione et devocione degustamus multitudinem laborum, contemtuum, derisionum et inproperiorum, nec[380] magnitudinem tormentorum et intensorum dolorum, que pro nobis ingratis servis tuis sustinuisti, ut nos a morte eriperes mortuosque[381] vivificares. Quia igitur tantum nos diligere dignatus es, tua[382] inmensam clemenciam pronis mentibus exoramus quatenus ob tue passionis et mortis reverenciam et tuorum clavorum piam conmemoracionem, peccatorum nobis veniam et vitam concedas sempiternam. **Responsus.** [48v] O quam beatum tormentum crudele, formidabile atque forte ulla absque pietate quantoque dolore plenum. P. Quando ministra infernales disconiungebant omnipotentem, cuius tormentum nobis celeste contulit premium. ℣. O bone Ihesu, intensos dolores in silencio tolerasti, quando penosas lacrimas ipse plorasti. P. Quando.

Leccio ii. O preciosi et gloriosi ac felices tres clavi de ferro materiali, quam[383] magna fuerit[384] virtus vestra. Non est cor quod cogitare, nec mens humana que conprehendere, nec lingua que enarare possit quomodo potentes fuistis resecare manus et pedes regis vite Christi Ihesu. Duricies enim et trucitas vestra fuit tam eficax que fecit cum[385] mori cum supremis et intensisimis doloribus. Regi cterno rupistis cutem et carnem, nervos et venas, intulistisque[386] ei mortem acerbam. Compullistis inocentem totum sui preciosissimi corporis [49r] sanguinem

---

[380] *nec:* + *non* interlinear.
[381] *mortuosque* + *e* with dots below to indicate removal.
[382] *tua:* read *tuam.*
[383] *quam:* the *u* is faded or erased and the *am* is lightly crossed out.
[384] *fuerit:* read *fuit.*
[385] *cum:* read *eum.*
[386] *intulistisque* + *e* with dots below to indicate removal.

effundere per firuras[387] et vulnera per quas vos multum crudeliter intrastis, et sic exanguem totaliter viribus destitutum et constrictum sumis doloribus, fecistis eum tradere spiritum Deo Patri. Set stupendum est valde quomodo rigorem vestrum non remisistis, et in molem materiam non fuistis mutati, ne ipse conditor nature, cui obedire debuistis, vestram acerbitatem in aliquo sentiret. Verum sentimos vos non esse de inobediencia nec de duricie vestra aut trucitate redarguendos. Credimus enim ipsum autorem[388] vite redenpcionem nostram operantem, sic disposuisse quod in propria vestra permaneretis natura et vestram retineretis duriciem ut crudelius pro nobis vulneratus dilectionem suam evidencius ostenderet.

Ideoque benedictum sit ferrum de quo fuistis fabricati, et benedicatur ipsa vestra duricies quam retinuistis, [49v] benedicti sint ictus maleorum qui vos penetrare conpulerunt menbra illa tam delicata[389] manus et pedes Redenptoris salvacionem nostram desiderabiliter operantis. Ea propter dulces et blandi ac multum amabiles estis predicandi propter magnitudinem vestre[390] excelencie. Quia digni fuistis infici[391] in menbra Redenptoris, et meruistis sustinere totum mundum in vobis pendentem. Ille ergo qui nos per vos redemit, ob vestri memoriam doloremque quos ad vestri rupturas in sumo sustinuit, propicietur nobis super magnitudinem peccatorum nostrorum. **Responsus.** O dulces et blandi, per universum mundum merito predicari debetis, o clavi, ex eo quod digni fuistis rumpere manus et pedes nostri Redemptoris. **P.** Duriciam vestram conservando in menbris nostri Salvatoris. ℣.[392] Meriti fuistis exaltari super angelorum coros dum in vobis sustinuistis Ihesum Regem celorum. [50r] **P.** Duriciam vestram.

Leccio tercia. O regina celi et mater piissima, quis intelligere et cognoscere ac contenplari possum magnitudinem multiplicium dolorum

---

[387] *firuras*: *fisuras*?
[388] *autorem*: *c* added above the *u*.
[389] *delicata*: *s* added at the end of the word.
[390] *vestre*: suppression mark over the final *e*.
[391] *infici*: *c* changed to *g*.
[392] ℣: a blot covers the letter.

quos tu, domina, mater Dei et hominis, ad pedem crucis passa fuisti tempore quo redempcio nostra in eadem consumabatur, cum visceraliter et penose intuebaris dedecora et supplicia, dolores et penas ac mortem turpissimam quam dilectissimus filius tuus pro redempcione nostra paciebatur, quem tu, domina, supreme diligebas, quem tu de Spiritu Sancto concepisti, quem sine dolore peperisti virginitate tua inviolata permanente, quem tu ut vera mater ubere de celo pleno lactasti, quem Deum et Redemptorem tuum vere et firmiter credidisti, eique triginta tribus annis familiariter et reverenter servivisti, qui in te et circa te grandia et stupenda mirabilia monstravit, tibique [50v] ut vere et reverende matri humiliter obedivit? Aspiciebas enim tu, domina, indesinenter nimio cum dolore et inidicibili angustia tuum dulcem natum in cruce elevatum confixum tribus clavis et eisdem sustentatum ac totaliter disconiunctum, efundentem de se totum sui preciosissimi corporis sanguinem in nostram redempcionem, et cum decurrentis sanguinis gutte super caput tuum et corpus caderent, non est cor quod estimare, nec lingua que reffere³⁹³ possit quantum dolorem paciebaris. Cor enim tuum tunc fuit totaliter vulneratum sicut manus et pedes filii tui.

Credimus namque sine dubio quod illi tres clavi qui filium tuum in cruce transfixerunt te non peperrerunt, qui ymo propri in corde tuo fuerunt affixi cum illis propriis doloribus quos filius tuus paciebatur in tua propria carne quam de te asump/sit. [51r] Et sic confixa et afecta magnis et indicibilibus doloribus in supremo gradu super omnes filios hominum martirium sustulisti. Verum, reverendissima mater et domina, querere volumus et scire a tua suprema honestate, quomodo illa die qua filius tuus passus est et mortem sustinuit in cella tua non stetisti inclusa, quomodo ad civitatem tumultuosam existi et ivisti ad illum pavidum locum montem Calvarie, cum de more tuo non fuisset yre ad videndum homines suspendi nec crucifigi? Cur timor qui mulieres talia spectacula audiendo et multo magis videndo invadit te non proibuit?³⁹⁴ Cur tua virginalis pudicicia te non detinuit? Sentimus, domina, et pie credimus

---

³⁹³ *referre*: *r* added above second *r*.
³⁹⁴ *proibuit*: *h* added above *oi*.

die illa mores tuos amore naturali filii tui fuisse mutatos et cor tuum
fuisse alienatum a te et extra te totumque fuisse positum [51v] inter
oprobria et suplicia ac intensos dolores que omnia tu, domina, in spiritu
vidisti filium tuum passurum. Ideo coacta fuisti exire et omnibus astare
ne absencia tua eidem dilectissimo filio tuo penas et dolores augmentaret,
et ne te ecciam martirium deesset: et ut ipsius martirii tui dolores et
angustias amarissime gustares, abstinuisti, domina, magna cum paciencia
et provida dispensacione a clamoribus et querelis que aflictis et in
angustiis positis magna in parte sunt in remedium consolacionis. Piis
autem et maternis lacrimis credimus que ob uberrime tua viscera relaxasti
ut saltem tibi in tanta angustia et amaritudine posite aliquantulum
satisfaceres.

Domina et mater venerandissima, credimus cor tuum non solus fuisse
illis tribus clavis confixum, verum ecciam totaliter per medium [52r]
concisum cum filii tui supra modum aflicti vocem audisti dicentem:
"Mulier, ecce filius tuus."³⁹⁵ Set nunquid, domina, viscera tua non
fuerunt doloris gladio totaliter transverberata cum vidisti et audisti filium
tuum dilectissimum cum lacrimis et clamore valido proclamantem:
"Deus meus, Deus meus, ut quid dereliquisti me?"³⁹⁶ Et tradendo
spiritum dicentem: "In manus tuas, Domine, commendo spiritum
meum."³⁹⁷ O benedicta et piissima mater, lauderis et tu ab omnibus
generationibus que cum ferventi desiderio nostre redenptionis cum
indicibili paciencia voluntatem tuam voluntati creatoris tui conformasti
et ardentissima cum caritate prebuisti consensum nostre salvationi.
Meritis ergo tuis misereatur³⁹⁸ nostri qui in tua propria carne nos
redimere dignatus fuit. **Responsus.** O inmaculata domina et mater
intac/ta, [52v] beatam te dicent omnis generaciones quia cum urenti. **P.**
Quodam desiderio nostre redenptionis tuam conformasti voluntatem
actori³⁹⁹ nostre salvacionis. ℣. Ardenti karitate consensisti redenptionem

---

³⁹⁵ John 19:26.
³⁹⁶ Matthew 27:46 and Mark 15:34, also in 14v above.
³⁹⁷ Luke 23:46, also in 18v above.
³⁹⁸ *misereatur*: second *e* added interlinear.
³⁹⁹ *actori*: *u* added above *ac*.

nostram, magna cum paciencia tolerasti viscerum tuorum rupturam. **P.** Quodam. Gloria patri. Actori nostre. Te deum laudamus. Ut s̄[400] Crucifixus fuit Christus tribus clavis. ℞. Ut nos solveret a mortis vinculis. **In Laudibus. Antiphana.** Devote recolimus memoriam clavorum quibus confixus est Christus rex celorum. **Psalmus.** Dominus regnavit.[401] **Antiphana.** Crucifixus fuit Christus linguis Judeorum ante quam traderetur in manus impiorum. **Psalmus.** Jubilate.[402] **Antiphana.** Verus pelicanus occisus fuit in cruce ut filios quos occiderat suo sanguine vivificaret. Deus, Deus meus. **Antiphana.** O durissimi clavi, omnes vos benedicimus qui transfixistis manus e pedes[403] agni inmaculati.[404] **P.** Benedicite. **Antiphana.** Tribus clavis stabat Ihesus suspensus quando dixit matri sue: "Mulier, ecce filius tuus." [53r] **P.** Laudate Dominum. **Capitula.** Extensus est Christus in cruce et tribus clavis confixus ut tinctus sanguine, stollam suam vino et sanguine ove[405] pallium suum lavaret.

Hymnum

Agnus ablator criminum,
patri oblatus in cruce,
clavis confixus asperis,
sis tu nobis refugium.

Occisus tunc pro homine
tinctus fuisti sanguine,
stollam lavasti et palium
cruore ove optimo.

Matris tue dulcissime
pie rupisti viscera
dicendo sibi anxie:
"Ecce filius tuus."

Gloria tibi Domine
qui per clavorum.

---

[400] s̄: an unknown symbol. The Spanish version has ѵ̃.
[401] Psalm 92 or 96 used on Friday, or Psalm 98 used on Saturday at Lauds.
[402] Psalm 99 used at Sunday Lauds.
[403] *e pedes*: ink seepage obscures the reading.
[404] *inmacuculati* in the text.
[405] *ove*: unclear reading. An initial letter, possibly *h*, was scratched out. The same word occurs in the last line of the second stanza of the hymn that follows. There is no equivalent word in the Spanish version.

℣. Oblatus est Christus propter scelera nostra et propter iniquitates nostras confixus es in cruce. **Ad Benedictus. Antiphana.** Cum ergo acepisset Ihesus acetum dixit: "Consumatum est," et inclinato capite tradidit spiritum.[406] **Psalmus.** Benedictus.[407] **Oracio.** Omnipotens sempiterne Deus, respice humilium vota et presta ut per [53v] clavorum et vulnerum filii tui Domini nostri Ihesu Christi comemoracionem quam devote celebramus, vulnerum peccatorum nostrorum medelam et animarum solamen consequi mereamur. Per eumdem. **A[408] Prima. Antiphana.** Devote recolimus. ℞. Ihesu Christe, Filii Dei vivi. **P.** Propter honorem trium clavorum miserere nobis. Gloria patri. **Ad Missam Officium.**[409] Nos autem gloriari opportet in clavis et cruce Domini nostri Ihesu Christi in quo es[410] salus, vita et resureccio nostra, per quem salvati et liberati sumus. ℣. Deus misereatur nostri et benedicat nobis: illuminet vultum suum super nos et misereatur nostri.[411] Gloria patri. Nos autem gloriari opportet in cruce et clavis Domini nostri Ihesu Christi in quo est salus, vita et resureccio nostra, per quem salvati et liberati sumus. Kyrie eleison. Christe eleison. Kyrie eleison. Gloria in excelsis Deo. **Oracio.** Omnipotens senpiterne Deus, respice humilium vota et presta [54r] ut per clavorum et vulnerum filii tui Domini nostri Ihesu Christi comemoracionem quam devote celebramus, vulnerum peccatorum nostrorum medelam et animarum solamen consequi mereamur. Per eumdem. **Lecio Isaie[412] prophete.** In diebus illis dixit Ysaias: Domine, quis

---

[406] John 19:30, Magnificat antiphon for Good Friday Vespers.
[407] Psalm 143 used at Saturday Vespers.
[408] *A*: very faint *d* added interlinear.
[409] The introit for Holy Thursday's mass follows, with the addition of *clavis et*.
[410] *es*: *t* added at end.
[411] Psalm 66:2.
[412] Isaiah 53:1-10, 12 b-d. *Isaie*: second *i* changed to *y* here and in the next occurrence.

ascendit sicut virgultum coram eo et sicut radix de tera[413] sicienti. Non est ei species neque decor et vidimus eum et non erat aspectus et consideravimus[414] despectum et novissimum virorum, virum dolorum et scientem infirmitatem et quasi absconditus vultus eius et despectus, unde nec reputavimus eum. Vere langores nostros ipse tulit et dolores nostros ipse portavit. Et nos putavimus eum quasi leprosum et percussum a Deo [et] humiliatum.[415] Ipse autem vulne/ratus [54v] est propter iniquitates nostras, actrictus[416] est propter scelera nostra. Disciplina pacis nostre super eum et livore eius sanati sumus. Omnes nos quasi oves erravimus, unusquisque in viam suam declinavit et Dominus posuit in eo iniquitatem omnium nostrum. Oblatus est quia ipse voluit et non aperuit os suum. Sicut ovis ad occisionem ducetur et quasi agnus coram tondente se obmutescet et non aperiet os suum. De angustia et de iudicio sublatus est. Generacionem eius quis enarabit, quia abcisus est de terra vivencium, propter scelus populi mei percussi eum? Et dabit impios pro sepultura et divites pro morte sua, eo quod iniquitatem non fecit nec inventus est dolus in ore eius. Et Dominus voluit conterere eum in infirmitate. Si posuerit pro peccato animam suam videbit semen lon/gevum [55r] et voluntas Domini in manu eius dirigetur,[417] pro eo quod tradidit in mortem animam suam et cum sceleratis reputatus est. Et ipse pecata[418] multorum tulit et pro transgressoribus oravit ut non perirent, dicit Dominus omnipotens. ℣. Christus factus est.

Alleluya ℣. Dulce lignum, dulces clavos, dulcia ferens pondera que sola fuisti digna sustinere regem celorum et Dominum. **Alleluya** ℣. Felix miles qui lancea quintum apperuit ostium ne deesset quinta porta ad peccatorum confugium.

Secundum Ioha[n]em.[419] In illo tempore stabant autem iuxta crucem

---

[413] *tera*: another *r* added interlinear.
[414] *consideravimus*: + *eum* in the margin.
[415] *humiiliatum* in the text.
[416] *actrictus*: *attritus*.
[417] Verses 11-12a omitted, perhaps due to the repetition of *pro eo quod*.
[418] *pecata*: *c* added above *ec*.
[419] John 19:25-30.

Ihesu mater eius et soror matris eius Maria Cleophe et Maria Magdalene. Cum vidisset ergo Ihesus matrem et discipulum stantem quem diligebat, dicit matri sue: "Mulier, ecce filius tuus." Deinde dicit discipulo: "Ecce mater tua." Et ex illa hora accepit eam discipulus in suam. [55v] Postea sciens Ihesus quia iam omnia consumata sunt, ut consumaretur scriptura dicit: "Sicio." Vas ergo positum erat aceto plenum. Illi autem spongiam plenam aceto ysopo circumponentes obtulerunt ori eius. Cum ergo accepisset Ihesus accetum, dixit: "Consumatum est." Et inclinato capite tradidit spiritum.

Credo. Ofrenda. Illi autem spongiam plenam aceto ysopo circumponentes obtulerunt ori eius. Cum ergo accepisset acetum noluit bibere.

Secreta. Beneplacita sit in conspectu tuo, Domine Ihesu Christe, Redemptor mundi, nostre devocionis oblacio quam in commemoracione clavorum et vulnerum tuorum oferimus exorantes ut sic pro tuis crucifixoribus exorasti ita nos tue redenpcionis facias esse consortei. Qui vivis.

Comunicanda. Hora autem nona clamavit Ihesus [56r] voce magna dicens: "Deus meus, Deus meus, ut quid derelequisti me?"[420] Et inclinato capite emisit spiritum. **Post comendon.**[421] Omnipotens senpiterne Deus, qui habundancia dilectionis tue unicum filium tuum pro redempcione nostra nocencium manibus tradi et in cruce clavis configi voluisti, concede nobis propicius ut per merita passionis eius restitutam nobis celestem hereditatem actingere valeamus. Qui tecum.

Ad Tercia. Antiphana. Crucifixus fuit Christus. **Capitula.** Extensus est Christus in cruce. Ry. O felicissimi clavi passionis Christi. V̷. Qui medicina vulnerorum nostrorum fuistis. P. Alleluya, alleluya. Gloria Patri. P. O felicisimi. V̷. Oblatus est quia ipse voluit. Ry. Et cum malediceretur non respondebat.

A Sexta. Antiphana. Verus pelicanus occisus fuit. **Capitula.** Michi autem absit gloriari nisi in clavis et cruce Domini nostri Ihesu

---

[420] Matthew 27:46, Mark 15:34.
[421] *comendon*: post-communion prayers are usually called *post communionem* or *ad complendum*. In this text, *comendon* is used here and on 72r, but *post communicanda* on 44r.

64

Christi per quem michi [56v] mundus crucifixus est et ego mundo,[422] Deo gracias. ℟. Oblatus est quia Christe voluit. ℣. Et cum malediceretur non respondebat. ℣. Tradidit in mortem animam suam. ℟. Et cum iniquis deputatus est. **Ad Nonam. Antiphana.** Tribus clavis. **Capitula.** Atendite qui proprio filio suo non pepercit Deus. Set pro nobis omnibus tradidit illum.[423] Deo gracias. Tradidit in. ℣. Et cum iniquis deputatus est. Gloria. **P.** Tradidit in mortem. ℣. Oblatus est Christus propter scelera nostra. ℟. Et propter iniquitates nostras confixus est in cruce. **In secundis Vesperis. Ad Magnificat. Antiphana.** Aspiciens mestissima mater extintum filium de cruce deponi brachia extendit ut caput ipsis suis manibus reciperet. **P.** Magnificat. **Ad secundum Complectorum. Super psalmus antiphana.** Planctu facto, cum flectibus et amaritudine traditum est corpus Ihesu aliene sepulture. **Ad Nunc Dimitis. Antiphana.** Mulieres sedentes ad monumentum amare lamentabantur Dominum.[424] [57r] **Nunc Dimitis. In Octavis. Invitatorium.** Nazarenum crucifixum venite adoremus. **Ad Benedictus. Antiphana.** Gloria, laus et honor sit tibi, Rex Christe Redenptor, qui in cruce clavatus peccata nostra portasti et in morte Deo Patri spiritum comendasti. **Ad Magnificat. Antiphana.** O preciosissime sanguis agni inmaculati. Qui per rupturas et tam afluenter multiplicatus existi per vulnera Christi crucifixi. O Magnificat. **Antiphana.** Domine rex virtutum, qui propter magnitudinem peccatorum nostrorum voluisti sputum vultum tuum a Iudcis, miserere nobis. **Psalmus.** Domine, Dominus noster.[425] **Antiphana.** Benedicamus pacienciam Ihesu qui ocultavit divinam potenciam suam crucis tormentum pro redemptione nostra super se portando. **Psalmus.** In Domino confido.[426] **Antiphana.** Corpus meum dedi percucientibus

---

[422] Galatians 6:14 with the addition of *clavis et.*
[423] Romans 8:32.
[424] Benedictus antiphon for Holy Saturday.
[425] Psalm 8 at Sunday Matins.
[426] Psalm 10 at Sunday Matins.

et genas meas vellentibus.⁴²⁷ **Psalmus.** Salvum me fac, Domine.⁴²⁸ ℣.
Oblatus est quia ipse voluit. **Responsus.** O ardentissima caritas
dileccioque supre/ma, [57v] que Christum martirizasti martirio trium
durissimorum clavorum. ℣. Filios ire⁴²⁹ redemistis et reconciliastis Deo
Patri rebelles et ingratos peccatores. **P.** Martirio. Gloria Patri. **P.**
Durissimorum. **Responsus.** O agnus innocens, qui proprio amore
generis humani cum silencio et sine murmure sustinuisti gravissimas
penas et intensissimos dolores mortis, miserere nobis. ℣. Tu qui
dignatus es crucifigi et mori in loco horroris et solitudinis. **Psalmus.**
Miserere.⁴³⁰ **Responsus.** Flagelato Ihesu et tradito ut crucifigeretur,
nullus fuit qui eius misereretur. Set quesita sunt sine mora illa
istrumenta quibus templum illud repente destrueretur. ℣. Parata est crux
de ligno salutifero. Fabricati sunt clavi de materiali ferro. **P.** Quibus
templum. **Antiphana.** Faciem meam non averti ab increpantibus
conspuentibus in me. ℣. Usque quo, Domine? **Antiphana.** Fixerunt
manus meas et pedes meos, dinumeraverunt omnia ossa mea.⁴³¹
Psalmus. Domine, quis [58r] habitabit?⁴³² **Antiphana.** Proprio filio
suo non pepercit Deus set pro nobis omnibus tradidit illum. **Psalmus.**
Deus, in adiutorium meum intende.⁴³³ ℣. Tradidit in mortem animam
suam. **Responsus.**⁴³⁴ O Fili Dei redenptor mundi, quantum nos
peccatores diligere dignatus es cum pro vita nostra et liberacione te in
cruce tribus clavis configi, in ea mori voluisti. ℣. Matrem tuam clavis
tu⁴³⁵ passionis ecciam martirizari permisisti. **P.** Te in cruce. Gloria
Patri. **P.** Et in ea mori voluisti. **Responsus.** Avete, preciosissime
plage Christi Ihesu, fuistis enim in suo corpore formate pulchre, de

---

⁴²⁷ Isaiah 50:6.
⁴²⁸ Psalm 11 at Sunday Matins.
⁴²⁹ *ire: irae.*
⁴³⁰ Psalm 50, 55, or 56 at Tuesday or Wednesday Matins.
⁴³¹ Psalm 21:17-18.
⁴³² Psalm 14 at Sunday Matins.
⁴³³ Psalm 69 at Thursday Matins and Holy Thursday.
⁴³⁴ The remainder of this folio is extremely difficult to read, especially the right half.
⁴³⁵ *tu: c or e added interlinear.*

66

suisque menbris recepistis. Valorem preciosissimum super lapides preciosos. **P.** Omnes vos adoramus et benedicimus in eternum. ℣. Ille qui vos propter nos recepit vestra nobis indulgeant virtute. **P.** Omnes vos adoramus. Gloria Patri. **P.** Dominus. **Responsus.** Lancea virtuosa, ferum[436] durum et [58v] crudele, necas eos quos tangis homines sic letifero. Cum veneno vulnerasti Christum pacientem et matrem condolentem.[437] **P.** Et liberasti a morte populum credentem. ℣. Mortuis propter peccatorum eternam vitam dedisti, ostium[438] glorie credentibus aperuisti. **P.** E liberasti a morte.

Los responsos sean de dezir por esta orden: flagelato, o agnus, o ardentissima, lancea, o Fili Dei Redemptor, avete.[439]

EL ROMANCE DE LAS MESMAS ORAS DE LOS CLAVOS

O fortíssimos clavos, todos vos bendecimos porque fuestes poderosos de ronper las manos e los pies del cordero sin mancilla, Ihesu Cristo crucificado. **Psalmus.** Laudate *cum reliquis.* **Capitula.** O muy más delicados braços e piernas reales, que con crueldat[440] firviente e fortaleza maravillosa, sofristes ser descoyuntadas por las manos de los crueles con cordeles ásperos. **Responso:** O ardentíssima caridat e amorío supremo, la qual martirizaste a Ihesu Cristo [59r] por martirio de tres duríssimos clavos. ℣. Los fijos de ira tú redemiste e reconciliaste a Dios Padre los peccadores desagradecidos e desobedientes. **P.** Por martirio. Gloria. De[441] clavos duríssimos.

Hympnum. Eterno Rey, muy más alto Padre de la gloria superna, todos te adoramos porquel fijo tuyo feciste redemptor de los omnes. O amor maravilloso, el qual posiste el fijo tuyo por los siervos en las

---

[436] *ferum*: a letter, possibly *u*, written in above *er*. Should read *servum*.
[437] *et . . . condolentem*: an insert written in the top margin.
[438] *ostium*: *h* added at the beginning.
[439] The responses in the Spanish version below correspond to the Latin responses given in the Octave but not in this order.
[440] *crueldat*: read *caridat*.
[441] *De*: preceded by *Dum,*. plus a small space.

manos de sus enemigos para que en la cruz dél fuesse fecho sacrificio. Enciende fuego cordial del tu grandíssimo amor en nosotros siervos tuyos por que a ti non seamos desagradecidos. Ihesu, verdadero pelicano, todos te bendezimos porque quando viste los fijos tuyos muertos, por los vivificar, ronpiste tus entrañas. A nos, vivificados por la tu sangre preciosa, acata con cara piado/sa, [59v] deféndenos con la tu potencia por que non perescamos en la batalla. Gloria sea a ti, Señor, el qual diste la tu bendicha sangre en precio de nuestra redempción por las llagas de los clavos.[442]

℣. O muy más bien aventurados clavos de la passión de Ihesu Cristo. ℞. Los quales fustes medicina de nuestras llagas. **Ad Magnificat. Antiphana.** O preciosíssima sangre del cordero sin mancilla, el qual saliste tan abondosamente e tan multiplicado por las ronpeduras de las llagas de Nuestro Señor Ihesu Cristo crucificado. Magnificat. **Oracio.** Todo poderoso.

Ad Conpletam. Crucificado fue Ihesu Cristo Nuestro Señor en la cruz por redemir e reconciliar los sus enemigos a Dios Padre.

Hymnum. Dulces clavos e amábiles, tanto duros e quanto ásperos, fecistes llagas a Ihesu Cristo Nuestro Señor, ronpiendo las manos e los pies del Salvador. Osados fuestes [60r] ronper los mienbros reales de Ihesu Cristo Nuestro Señor, vencedor del enemigo, destruidor del su señorío. Ihesu, Salvador del siglo, palabra del Padre altíssimo, a nosotros que fazemos comemoración de los tus clavos, guárdanos de la boca del infierno. Gloria sea a ti.

Ad Nunc Dimitis. Antiphana. Ihesu Cristo Nuestro Señor fue fecho obediente fasta el duro traspasamiento de los clavos e fasta el cruel tormento de la cruz.

Ad Matutinam. Invitate. Adoremos al Señor, Rey crucificado por

---

[442] The hymns in the Spanish version of the Hours of the Nails lack indications for line endings and do not lend themselves to rendition in poetic form.

nos en la cruz, de tres clavos colgado. Venite adoremus, venite exultemus Domino.[443]

Hympnus. O Padre de la lumbre eterna, plasmador santo del omne, pues que redemiste la tu fechura, perdona a nosotros míseros. O Fijo e príncipe muy más noble, vencedor de la batalla de Sathanás, conserva a nos, siervos tuyos, por la tu sangre [60v] preciosa redemidos. Piadoso redemtor de la humilde naturaleza flaca e caída, en las hondas e trabajos de esta vida, sey[444] acerca de nos.[445] Ronpe con los clavos las entrañas de nuestra carne mortífera por que nosotros, en este mundo crucificados, en el otro alcançemos los bienes celestiales. Gloria sea a ti.

In primo Nocturno. Antiphana. Ordenaste, muy más piadoso Padre, el fijo tuyo ignocente ser traído en las manos de los pecadores por nuestra rede[m]pción, aleluya. **Psalmo**. Beatus vir qui non habit.[446] **iiª antiphana**. O cordero ignocente, Ihesu Cristo redemptor, el qual en la cruz de tres clavos estoviste colgado por redempción de los tus siervos, aleluya. **Psalmo**. Domine, quid multi. **iij antiphana**. O muy más piadosa madre e virgen non tañida, la qual fuste traspasada de aquellos tres clavos en los quales viste el fijo tuyo colgado, aleluya. **Psalmo**. Cum invocare.[447] ℣. Vulneratus est Christus[448] iniquitates nostras, aleluya. Et langores nostros ipse portavit, aleluya.

[61r] **Leccio prima**. O bone Ihesu, por quantos e por quan inextimábiles modos todo enteramente te diste a nosotros indignos

---

[443] *Venite . . . Domino*: Psalm 94. Although the word *Psalmus* or *Psalmo* is not usually included in the Spanish version, the psalms are readily recognizable, as the incipits are given in Latin. Other rubrics may also be omitted or changed. Scriptural references already noted in the Latin version will not be repeated in the Spanish version.

[444] *sey*: ant. *sé.*

[445] *acerca de nos*: I have transcribed the Latin on 45v as *propicius*; however, the uncertainty of the reading due to abbreviation, word division, ink blots, and faded letters may account for this Spanish rendition, perhaps of *propius*.

[446] *habit*: *abiit.*

[447] *invocare*: *invocare[m].*

[448] *Christus*: + abbreviation for *propter* added interlinear.

siervos, verdaderamente non abastó[449] al tu ardentíssimo amor, el qual veniste a nos demostrar, tú del cielo en la tierra aver descendido, e cubriendo la tu incomprehensíbile divinidat con el manto de la nuestra carne mortal, e ansí te demostraste a los ojos de los mortales. Mas la tu linpia e preciosa sangre, para lavar las manzillas de los nuestros pecados, en la tu tierna edad enpeçaste a deramar. Verdaderamente quesiste demostrar a nosotros el profectíssimo[450] grado del tu buen amor; sin engaño ninguno toviste por bien de nos amar quando, non tan solamente por los amigos, mas tanbién por tus enemigos, muy desonradamente padesciste muy cruel passión, la qual por muerte angustiosa te fizo dar el spíritu. [61v] O Señor, ¿quién se podría contener de gemir e llorar si con los ojos corporales devotamente te acatara, quando Señor, Rey de los cielos, demostrándote ser verdadero omne, temiste la espantable muerte a ti aparejada? E con temor della en la oración humilde que al Padre feciste, en tanta agonía e trabajo fueste puesto quel tu sudor fue fecho ansy commo sudor de sangre en la tiera[451] corriente. Mas aunque la tu linpia e delicada carne fue enferma e la tu sensualidat se arredrava de la passión, mas el tu spíritu permanesció triunphante e vencedor. E assí, Señor, con la obediencia perfectíssima del tu Padre e con la nuestra soberana dilectión, tú, eterna vida, de buena voluntad te ofreciste a la muerte, la tu voluntad con la voluntad del tu Padre conformando, e entonces, con fortaleza non vencible, en el huerto tus enemigos esperaste.

O inestimable [62r] amor de la tu caridat, dulcíssimo Ihesu, que quesiste tú ser muerto por redemir al siervo, non oviste miedo a los gentiles armados, nin a los acusantes, nin a los ministros a ti ofendientes e injuriantes, nin aboreciste de ellos ser atado, e atado, ser traído delante de los sacerdotes e delante del juez Poncio Pilato, el qual sobre ti dio sentencia de muerte en la cruz e te puso en las manos de tus enemigos. Mas, o amantíssimo Ihesu, ¿de çolloços e sospiros quién cessar deve, en

---

[449] *abastó*: ant. *bastó*, " to be sufficient."

[450] *profectíssimo*: *ro* crossed out and a suppression mark added to the stem of the *p* changing the reading to *perfectíssimo*.

[451] *tiera*: another *r* added interlinear.

como él acatasse con los sus ojos a ti, Señor, Rey de los siglos, mancebo valiente, flor de toda carne, sin color e semejança de omne trayente contra[452] el monte de Calvaria ponderoso palo de cruz, en el qual avías de padescer muerte? Esso mesmo,[453] Señor buen Ihesu, non siento coraçón que non fuera quebrantado quando [a] aquel [62v] lugar espantable tú, fatigado e cansado, llegaste menospreciado, abierto,[454] escarneçido, de tus ropas despojado el tu cuerpo precioso a vista de todo el pueblo, puesto en las manos de tus enemigos, e sin porfía e sin resistencia ninguna, los tus braços reales estendiste e las tus delicadas manos humilmente abriste. E los tus santíssimos pies aparejaste para que los tus enemigos en ti cunpliesen toda su mala voluntat. E la tu boca santíssima cerrada e apretada, sofriste ronpeduras tan dolorosas e llagas atan[455] crueles de tres clavos duros, los quales con enpetuosos[456] golpes cruelmente rasgaron e penetraron el cuero, carne, nervios e venas de las manos e de los pies tuyos.

Mas nosotros, miserábiles fijos de maldición, con gran ceguedat e con grannt menosprecio e vanidat [63r] de desagradecimiento, non cognoscemos[457] el tu tan grandíssimo amor nin sentimos los tus innumerábiles beneficios, llenos de espanto,[458] dignos de admiración, ca non gustamos[459] con atención nin devoción la muchedunbre de los tus trabajos, menosprecios e[460] escarnios e denuestos. Nin pensamos la grandeza de los tormentos e dolores intensos que por nos desagradecidos siervos tuyos sofriste por nos librar de la muerte e muertos vivificar. Pues que ansí es, Señor, que tanto toviste por bien de nos amar, a la tu inmensa clemencia, prostados[461] en el suelo, humilmente suplicamos que

---

[452] *contra*: *r* written above the word, ant. "towards."
[453] *Esso mesmo*: *asimismo*.
[454] *abierto*: read *abiecto*.
[455] *atan*: ant. *tan*.
[456] *enpetuosos*: *impetuosos*, i.e., *con ímpetu*, "violent."
[457] *cognoscemos*: ant. *conocemos*, "recognize or understand."
[458] *espanto*: "astonishment, wonder."
[459] *gustamos*: "be acquainted with, experience."
[460] *e*: repeated.
[461] *prostados*: metathesized form of *postrados*.

por reverencia de la tu muerte e passión e de los clavos piadosa comemoración, a nos quieras dar perdonança[462] de los nuestros pecados e vita sempiterna por siempre jamás, amén. **Responso**. O cordero ignocente, el qual por amorío proprio del linage huma/no, [63v] con silencio e sin murmuración soportaste penas gravíssimas e dolores intenssos de muerte, ave merçed de nosotros. Tú, el qual toviste por bien de ser crucificado e morir en el lugar de espanto e soledat, ave merçed de nos.

Leccio secunda. O preciosos e gloriosos e más bien aventurados tres clavos de fiero material, o quán grande fue la vuestra virtud. Non ay coraçón que lo pensar pueda, nin entendimiento humano que lo pueda conprehender[463] cómo fuestes poderosos de rasgar las manos e los pies de Ihesu Christo, rey de vida. Ciertamente la vuestra dureza e crueldat fue tan eficaç que le fizo morir con soberanos e intensos dolores. Al rey eterno ronpistes el cuero, la carne, los nervios et venas, causando en él muerte muy cruel, constreñistes al inocente derramar toda la sangre del su cuerpo precioso de las llagas e ronpeduras, por las quales [64r] vos cruelmente entrastes. E ansí desangrado e de todas las fuerças afloxado, constreñido con grandes dolores le fecistes dar el spíritu a Dios Padre. Set stupendum est, mas mucho nos avemos de espantar, cómmo non perdistes el vuestro rigor, e non fustes en materia blanda trasmudados en tal manera quel fazedor de la naturaleza, al qual vos avés[464] de obedecer, por ningún modo non sintiera la vuestra dureza. Verdaderamente creemos vos non ser merecedores de rephrensión[465] por la vuestra dureza, desobediencia, o crueldat porque creemos el mesmo autor de vida, obrante la nuestra redenpción, ansí lo aver ordenado que vos permaneciessedes[466] en la vuestra propia naturaleza, reteniendo la vuestra dureza, por quel Salvador, más cruelmente llagado por vos, con mayor evidencia nos demostrase el su infinito amor.

---

[462] *perdonança*: ant. *perdón*, "pardon" or "indulgence."

[463] *conprehender*: ant. *comprender*.

[464] *avés*, archaic *avedes*: *habéis*.

[465] *rephrensión*: read *reprensión*.

[466] *permaneciessedes*: ant. *permanecieseis*.

E por ende bendicho sea [64v] el fiero del qual vos fustes fabricados. E bendicha sea la vuestra dureza que retovistes. Bendichos sean los golpes de los martillos que vos constriñeron penetrar los mienbros tan delicados, manos e pies del nuestro Redentor, obrante con grandíssimo deseo la nuestra salvación. Por lo qual, dulces, blandos e dignos de mucho amor, devés[467] por todo el mundo ser predicados por la grandeza de la vuestra exelencia e dignidat, por quanto fustes dignos de ser fincados en los mienbros de nuestro Redemptor e merescistes sostener, encima de vos colgado, aquel que todo el mundo tiene en la mano. Pues que ansí es aquel que a nos redimió por vos, por memoria vuestra e de los dolores que recibió en grado sumo de las vuestras ronpeduras, perdone a nosotros la grandeza de los nuestros peccados. Tu autem.[468] Tú, Señor, ave merced de nos. **Responso.** [65r] Açotado el buen Ihesu, en el monte de Calvario puesto, non fue ninguno que oviese del pieadat[469] nin misericordia, mas sin tardança ninguna fueron buscados aquellos instrumentos con los quales aquel tenplo santo muy ayna[470] fuesse destruido. ℣. Aparejada es la cruz de palo salutífero, fabricados son los clavos de material fiero. **P.** Con los quales aquel tenplo sancto fue destruydo.

Leccio iijª. O reyna del cielo e madre muy más piadosa, ¿quién podría entender, cognoscer o considerar la grandeza de los multip[l]icados dolores, los quales tú, madre del buen Ihesu, Dios e omne verdadero, al pie de la cruz padesciste el tienpo que la nuestra redenpción se obrava, quando cordialmente[471] e con mucha pena acatavas los tormentos, dolores, penas, denuestos e turpíssima muerte, los quales el tu dulce e mucho amado fijo por la nuestra redenpción de propia voluntad padecía; al qual tú, [65v] Señora, soberanamente amavas; el qual tú, Señora, de Spíritu Sancto conçebiste; al qual sin dolor pariste,

---

[467] *devés*: *debéis*.

[468] *Tu autem*: a standard phrase that marks the end of the reading. The full text would be: *Tu autem, Domine, miserere nobis.*

[469] *pieadat*: *piedad.*

[470] *ayna*: ant. "quickly."

[471] *cordialmente*: "felt in the innermost being."

la tu virginidat non tañida en ti permaneciente; al qual tú, ansí commo verdadera madre, con leche celestial lo criaste; el qual redenptor e Dios tuyo verdadera e firmemente lo creíste; al qual treinta e tres años familiarmente e con mucha reverencia serviste; el qual en ti e açerca[472] de ti infinitos e grandes miraglos[473] e maravillosos demostró; a ti, ansí commo a verdadera madre con mucha reverencia e humildat sienpre obedesció? Miravas tú, Señora, continuamente con grandíssimo dolor e con angustia indicíbile[474] al tu dulce fijo en la cruz elevado, todo descoiuntado, de tres clavos colgado, de sí deramante toda la sangre del su cuerpo precioso en precio de nuestra redenpción. E quando tú sentías las gotas de sangre sobre tu cabeça [66r] coriente, non siento yo coraçón que pueda pensar nin lengua que pueda contar quánto era el dolor que tú, piadosa madre, padecías. El tu coraçón en esse tienpo fue todo llagado, ansí commo las manos e los pies del tu fijo.

Creemos verdaderamente sin dubda que aquellos tres clavos que en la cruz al tu fijo traspasaron, a ti non perdonaron. Mas propiamente dentro en tu coraçón fueron fincados con aquellos mesmos dolores, los quales el fijo tuyo en la tu propia carne padesçía, la qual de ti verdaderamente avía tomado. E ansí traspasada e quebrantada con muy grandes e indicíbiles dolores en grado soberano[475] todos los fijos de los omnes martirio reçebiste. Verum credimus verdaderamente, reverendísima Madre e Señora, de la tu suprema onestad queremos saber ¿por qué aquel día quel fijo tuyo [66v] padescía, reçibiendo tan cruel muerte, non estoviste en casa encerada, mas saliste a la çibdat toda escandalizada e turbada, e fueste [a] aquel espantable lugar, monte de Calvarie, en commo la costunbre tuya non fuesse de ver los omnes muertos, crucificados, nin aforcados? ¿Por quél temor que a las mugeres retrae[476] a ti non detovo aquel día de ver tan grandes crueldades,

---

[472] *açerca*: ant. *cerca*.

[473] *miraglos*: ant. *milagros*.

[474] *indicíbile*: *indecible*.

[475] *soberano*: the meaning of the sentence indicates that *sobre* must be read here, just as *super* is included in the Latin version on 51r.

[476] *retrae*: supression mark over the final *e*.

señaladamente en el fijo tuyo? ¿Por qué, Señora, la tu linpia virginidat non te detuvo? Sentimos, Señora, e piadosamente creemos aquel día las costunbres e condiciones ser mudadas por amor natural del tu fijo, e el tu coraçón ser agenado[477] de ti, puesto totalmente en medio de tantos oprobrios,[478] denuestos, tormentos e dolores intensos, los quales tú, Señora, en spíritu conosçiste el tu fijo pa/decedero. [67r] E por ende tú fueste constreñida a salir de tu casa e ser presente a tantos dolores por que la tu absencia non acrecentase penas e dolores al tu fijo mucho amado. E aun por que a ti non fallesciese martirio, e por que más amargosamente gustases e sintiesses las angustias e dolores del tu martirio, con mucha paçiençia e muy sabia dispensación, tú, Señora, cesaste de las quexas e querellas, las quales a los aflictos e tribulados dan grannt parte de remedio e consolación. Mas creemos, Señora, que tú afloxaste[479] las entrañas del tu coraçón abondosamente de lágrimas maternales por satisfazer algunnt tanto a ti puesta en tanta angustia, amargura e tribulaçión.

O Señora, madre digna de mucha veneraçión, creemos el tu coraçón non tan solamente de tres clavos ser colgado, mas por medio, de todo en todo, [67v] ser partido, quando oystes[480] la boz del tu fijo tanto aflicto diziéndote a ti: "Muger, cata a tu fijo." ¿Quién dubda, Señora, que las tus entrañas non fueron cortadas con espadas de dolor quando viste e oíste al tu fijo mucho amado, con lágrimas e con muy grannt dolor, proclamante diziendo: "Dios mío, Dios mío, ¿por qué me dexaste?" E dio a Dios Padre todo poderoso el spíritu diziendo: "Señor, en las tus manos encomiendo el mi spíritu." O bendicha e muy más piadosa madre, mereçistes ser alabada de todas las generaçiones porque, con deseo ardentíssimo de la nuestra redempçión e con paciencia indicíbile, la tu voluntad con la voluntad del tu criador conformaste, e con caridat ferviente consentiste a la nuestra salvaçión. Por los tus méritos, aya merçed de nosotros el que en [68r] tu propia carne tovo por bien de nos

---

[477] *agenado*: ant. for *enagenado*, "estranged, alienated."
[478] *oprobrios*: *oprobios*.
[479] *afloxaste*: *aflojaste*, "eased."
[480] *oystes*: final *s* crossed out.

75

redemir. **Responso**. O Fijo de Dios e redemptor del mundo, quánto toviste por bien de amar a nos los pecadores en commo por la vida nuestra e liberación tú quessiste en la cruz con tres clavos ser enclavado e en ella ser muerto. ℣. La madre tuya con los clavos de la tu passión tan bien[481] quesiste que fuese martirizada. **P**. En commo tú en la cruz quesiste ser muerto e en ella de tres clavos ser colgado. Gloria Patri. E en la cruz ser muerto. Te Deum laudamus. ℣. Crucificado fue Ihesu Christo de tres clavos por desatar a nos de las cadenas de la muerte. **In Laudibus**. **Psalmo**. **Antiphana**. Devotamente celebramos la fiesta de los clavos, con los quales Ihesu Christo, rey de los çielos, fue crucificado. Crucificado fue Ihesu Christo por las lenguas de los judíos antes que fuesse traído en las manos de los malos. Jubilate. El verdadero pelicano [68v] fue muerto en la cruz por vivificar con la sangre suya los fijos que eran muertos. Deus, Deus meus. O duríssimos clavos, todos vos bendeçimos porque traspasastes las manos e los pies del cordero sin manzilla. Benedicite, omnia. De tres clavos está Ihesu Christo colgado, quando dixo a la madre suya: "Cata tu fijo." Laudate. **Capitula**, Estendido fue Ihesu Christo en la cruz e de tres clavos suspenso por que él, cubierto de sangre, pudiesse bien lavar el su manto e saya con agua e sangre.

Hypnum. O cordero, raedor[482] de los pecados, en la cruz al Padre ofreçido, de clavos ásperamente ronpido, sey tú, Señor, nuestro refugio. Muerto por entonces por redemir al omne, cubierto de sangre, lavaste la saya e el manto con agua e sangre del tu cuerpo coriente. Piadosamente ronpiste las entra/ñas [69r] de la madre tuya dulcísima, diziéndole angustiosamente: "Cata el fijo tuyo." Gloria sea a ti. ℣. Ofrecido es Ihesu Christo por nuestros pecados e por nuestras maldades en la cruz es enclavado. **Ad Benedictus**. **Antiphana**. En commo beviesse Ihesu Christo, Nuestro Señor, fiel[483] e vinagre dixo: "Acabado es." E abaxada la cabeça dio el spíritu al su Padre todo poderoso. Benedictus

---

[481] *tan bien*: *también*.
[482] *raedor*: the last four letters are squeezed into the space left by a previous erasure.
[483] *fiel*: *hiel*.

Dominus. **Oraçio**. Todo poderoso[484] Dios eterno.
Antiphana de Prima. Devotamente celebramos la comemoraçión de los clavos, en los quales Ihesu Christo, rey de los çielos, fue enclavado, aleluya. ♥. Ihesu Christo, fijo de Dios bivo, ave merçet de nos. ♥. Por honor de los tres clavos, ave merçed de nos. Gloria sea al Padre. ♥. Levántate, Señor, e ayúdanos por reve[re]ncia de los clavos.
Oficio de la Missa. A nosotros cunple ser glorificados en la cruz e en los clavos de Nuestro Señor Ihesu Christo, en el qual está la nuestra salud e redempción; por el qual somos salvos [69v] e libres. ♥. Dios aya merçed de nosotros e nos bendiga; demuestre la cara suya sobre nos e[485] aya merçed de nos. Gloria sea al Padre, e al Fijo en los clavos colgado, e al Spíritu Santo, ansí commo era en el prinçipio e es agora e será para sienpre e por todos los siglos de los siglos, amén. Kyrie eleison. Domine, miserere. Señor, ave merçed de nos. Christe eleison. Christe, exaudi nos. Señor ungido, oydnos. Kyrie eleison. Spiritus Sante Deus, miserere nobis. Spíritu Sancto, ave merçed de nos.
Oración. Todo poderoso Dios sempiterno, acata a las humildes peticiones de nosotros que te rogamos. E danos por la reverençia e comemoraçíon de las llagas e clavos del fijo tuyo Ihesu Christo, Nuestro Señor, a[486] qual devotamente oramos que merescamos alcançar consolaçión de nuestras culpas e pecados, por el mérito de Ihesu Christo, Nuestro Señor, en la [70r] cruz cruçificado e enclavado; el qual bive e reyna contigo en unidad del Spíritu Santo por sienpre jamás, amén.
Epístola de Isaías. En aquellos días que Ysaías prophetizava, dixo: ¿Quién creyó lo que[487] oyó? E el braço del Señor, ¿a quién es revelado? Subió o nasçió ansí como piértegas[488] delante dél e ansí commo rayz de tiera seca, non es en él color nin semejança; vímosle e non tenía acatamiento de omne. E pensámosle ser menospreciado e postrero de

---

[484] *poderoso*: + *e*.
[485] *e*: + *a e* in the text.
[486] *a*: a letter, perhaps *l*, blotted out before the *a*; possibly metathesis of *al*.
[487] *que*: + *yo*.
[488] *piértegas*: ant. *pértiga*, "a long stick, a rod." The Vulgate uses *virgultum*, "a sprout."

todos los varones, varón de dolores e conosçedor de toda enfermedat. E la cara suya estava ansí commo abscondida[489] e menospreciada, por lo qual non le reputamos. Verdaderamente él truxo[490] las nuestras enfermedades, e los nuestros dolores él los soportó, e nos le pensamos ser ansí commo leproso, humillado e ferido de Dios. El fue llagado por las nuestras maldades e [70v] fue quebrantado por los nuestros pecados; el açote de nuestra paz fue puesto sobre él. E por el deramamiento de la su sangre todos somos sanos. Todos nosotros ansí commo ovejas eramos,[491] e cada uno de nos se apartó por su carera, e Dios puso en él el mal de todos nosotros. Fue ofreçido porque él quiso, e la boca suya non la abrió. Será traído a la muerte ansí commo oveja, e mudeçerá[492] ansí commo el cordero delante del desquilador, e la su boca non abrirá. De angustia e de juizio es tomado. La generaçión suya, ¿quién la podrá contar, porque fue cortado de la tierra de los bivientes? Por el pecado del mi pueblo, yo lo ferí. E dará los malos por sepultura, a los ricos por la muerte suya, por quanto non fizo maldat ninguna nin fue fallado engaño en su boca. E Dios le quiso quebrantar en enfermedat. E si posiere el ánima suya [7lr] por el pecado, verá la su generaçión muy luenga,[493] e la voluntad del Señor en su mano será endereçada, por quanto puso el ánima suya a la muerte, e con los malos e pecadores fue puesto; e él los pecados de muchos truxo, e por los traspasadores oró por que non pereçiesen. E esto dize el Señor todo poderoso.

Aleluya primera. Canta alabanças a Dios, tú, cruz de Ihesu Christo Nuestro Señor, traiente sobre ti todas las cosas dulçes e amorosas; dulçe es el palo, dulçes son los clavos. Canta alabanças a Dios porque tú sola fuste digna de sostener en ti al rey de los çielos e Señor. **Aleluya segunda.** O bien aventurado el cavallero que con su lança abrió el quinto postigo por que non faltasse la quinta puerta dada a los peccadores en refugium, aleluya.

---

[489] *abscondida*: ant. *escondida*.

[490] *truxo*: *trajo*.

[491] *eramos*: second *r* added interlinear.

[492] *mudeçerá*: ant. *enmudecer*.

[493] *luenga*: ant. *larga*.

Evangelium secundum Joanem. En aquel tienpo que predicava[494] Ihesu Christo, Nuestro Señor, padeçía,[495] estava[496] açerca [71v] de la cruz la su madre bendicha, e su ermana María Cleophe e santa María Magdalena. E commo vido Nuestro Señor la su madre stante e al diçiplo que él mucho amava, dixo a su madre: "Muger, cata tu fijo." Después dixo al deçiplo: "Cata tu madre." E desde aquella ora el diçiplo la tomó por madre suya. Después, sabiendo el buen Ihesu que todas las cosas eran acabadas, por que se cumpliese la escriptura, dixo Nuestro Señor: "E set."[497] Estava aparerado[498] un vaso lleno de vinagre. E los ministros fincheron[499] una esponja de aquel vinagre e pusiéronla a la boca de Nuestro Señor. En commo Nuestro Señor gustase aquel vinagre[500] dixo: "Acabado es." E inclinó la cabeça, dio el spíritu.

Credo in Deum. **Ofrenda**. Aquellos ministros pusieron[501] una esponja llena de fiel e vinagre a la boca de Nuestro Señor. E en commo lo gustó non lo quiso [72r] bever, aleluya.

Sacramenta. Señor Ihesu Christo, Redemptor del mundo, grata e bien apaçible sea la ofrenda de la nuestra redempción en el acatamiento de la tu divina magestat, la qual rogando ofreçemos en memoria de los clavos e llagas tuyas que ansí commo por tus crucifixores rogaste, ansí fagas a nosotros ser parçioneros de la tu redempción; el qual vives e reinas con Dios Padre, en unidat del Spíritu Sancto, por todos los siglos de los siglos, amén.

Comunicanda. A la ora de nona clamó Nuestro Señor Ihesu Christo, e dio una grant boz e dixo: "Dios mío, Dios mío, ¿por qué me desanparaste?" E abaxada la cabeça dio el spíritu. **Post comendon**. Todo poderoso, sempiterno Dios, el qual con grande abundançia del tu

---

[494] *predicava*: underlined and separated by a line from *Ihesu*.

[495] *que . . . padecía* are not found in the Latin version nor in John's gospel.

[496] *estava*: *va* added above the line.

[497] *E set*: *He* (in modern Spanish *tengo*) *sed*.

[498] *aparerado*: read *aparejado*.

[499] *fincheron*: from *henchir*, "to fill up."

[500] *vinagre*: *r* interlinear.

[501] *pusieron*: repeated.

amor, un solo fijo tuyo por la nuestra redempçíon quisiste ser enclavado
en la cruz con clavos e en las manos de los pecadores ser traído, [72v]
da a nos piadosamente que por los méritos de la su passión podamos
alcançar la heredat çelestial a nosotros restituida; él bive e reina contigo
por sienpre jamás, amén.
Antiphana de Terçia. Crucificado fue Ihesu Christo de las lenguas
de los judíos ante que fuesse puesto en las manos de los malos, aleluya.
Capitula. Extendió, et cetera. ℣. O feliçíssimos clavos de la passión
de Ihesu Christo, aleluya, aleluya; los quales fuestes medeçina de
nuestras llagas, aleluya, aleluya. Gloria sea al Padre, et cetera. **P.** O
felicíssimos clavos. ℣. Fue ofrecido porque él quiso, aleluya. E quando
le denostavan, non respondía, aleluya.
Antiphana de Sexta. El verdadero pelicano en cruz fue muerto por
vivificar con la su sangre a los sus fijos muertos. **Capitula.** A mí sea
menos ser glorificado salvo en la cruz e clavos de Nuestro Señor Ihesu
Christo, por el qual el mundo es a mí cruçificado e yo al mundo, Deo
graçias. ℣. Fue ofreçido por quél quisso, aleluya; [73r] e quando le
denostavan non respondía, aleluya, aleluya. Gloria sea. **P.** Fue
ofreçido. **P.** Puso el ánima suya a la muerte, aleluya, e con los malos
fue contado, aleluya.
Antiphana de Nona. De tres clavos estava Ihesu Christo Nuestro
Señor suspenso, quando dixo a su madre: "Muger, cata tu fijo," aleluya.
Capitula. Acatad que Dios non perdonó al propio fijo suyo, mas trúxole
a la muerte por todos nosotros, Deo graçias. ℣. Puso el ánima suya en
la muerte, aleluya, aleluya, e con los malfechores fue contado, aleluya,
aleluya. Gloria sea. **P.** Puso el ánima. ℣. Fue sacrificado el Christo
por nuestros pecados, aleluya, aleluya. E por nuestras maldades fue
enclavado, aleluya.
Antiphana a las ii^as Vísperas. Mirando la más triste madre al su
fijo muerto ser quitado de la cruz, estendió sus braços para lo reçebir,
aleluya. Manificat anima mea Dominum.
A las Cunpletas. Antiphana. Fecho un grant planto,[502] con
muchos lloros e con grande amargura es enterrado el cuerpo del buen

---

[502] *planto*: ant. *llanto con gemidos y sollozos.*

80

Ihesu en agena [73v] sepoltura, aleluya. **Ad Nunc Dimitis**. Las
mugeres asentadas al monumento amargosamente lloravan a Nuestro
Señor Ihesu Christo, aleluya. **Por la selmana.**⁵⁰³ **Invitatorium**. Al nazareno cruçificado venit
adoremus. **Antiphana de Beneditus**. Gloria e alabança e honrra sea a
ti, Rey Christe, Redemptor; el qual en cruz enclavado, nuestros pecados
troxiste, e en la muerte a Dios Padre el tu spíritu comendaste. **Ad
Magnificat**. Bendicha e muy onrrada, a ti, madre de Dios, alabamos
porque al pie de la cruz por los nuestros pecados el tu coraçón e
mienbros enflamaste e las tus entrañas quemantes así commo brasa biva,
e toda te transformaste en aquellas mesmas llagas del tu fijo, porque la
carne de anbos a dos⁵⁰⁴ es una, aleluya. **Super salmus antiphana**. O
Señor, rey de las virtudes, el qual por la grandeza de nuestros peccados
quesiste la tu cara ser escopida de los judíos, ave merçed de nos. **Otra
antiphana**. Bendigamos la paçiençia de Ihesu Christo, [74r] el qual
negó la su potençia, levando el tormento de la cruz sobre sí por nuestra
redempçión. **Responso**. O quám bienaventurado tormento cruel e
temeroso, fuerte sin piedat e quánto doloroso, quando los ministros
infernales descoyuntaron al poderoso, el tormento del qual dio a nos
premio celestial. ℣. O bone Ihesu, intensos dolores en silençio toleraste,
quando tan penosas e multiplicadas lágrimas lloraste. **Responso**. O sin
mancilla Señora, e madre non tañida, todas las generaçiones te dizen
bienaventurada, porque con quemante deseo de la nuestra redención, la
tu voluntad conformaste al autor de nuestra salvaçión. ℣. Por ardiente
caridat consentiste nuestra redem[p]çión,⁵⁰⁵ por gran paçiençia soportaste
ronpimiento de tus entrañas. **Responso**. Dulçes e blandos por todo el
mundo, o clavos, deves ser predicados, pues que fuestes dignos de
ronper las manos e los pies de nuestro Redemptor, [74v] guardando la
vuestra dureza en los mienbros de nuestro Salvador. ℣. Mereçistes ser
ençalçados sobre los coros de los ángeles quando sostovistes en vos al
Rey, Ihesu Christo. **Responso**. Lança virtuosa, siervo duro e cruel,

⁵⁰³ *selmana*: *semana*.
⁵⁰⁴ *anbos a dos*: pleonasm for *ambos*.
⁵⁰⁵ *redem[p]çión*: a letter erased after *m*.

matas los omnes que tañes, ansy como venino[506] mortal, llagaste a Christo paçiente. Libraste de la muerte al pueblo creyente. ꝟ. A los muertos en pecado eterna vida diste; puerta de gloria a los creyentes abriste. [**Responso**.] Dios vos salve, llagas de Ihesu Christo preçiosas, en su cuerpo fustes formadas fermosas, de los sus mienbros reçebistes grande valor sobre las piedras preçiosas. Todos vos adoramos e bendeçimos por sienpre. ꝟ. Aquel que vos reçibió por nos, por vuestra virtud dé perdón.

Suplicación. Señor, Dios poderoso, Ihesu Christo Redemptor, tú que por tu preçiosa sangre redemiste mi ánima, Señor, por tu abondosa clemençia, ave merçet de mí. E dame graçia e virtud que yo [75r] biva e muera en tu sancta fe, creyendo, confessando, afirmando los quatorze artículos[507] bien e conplidamente quanto perteneçe a mi salvaçión. Yo, desde agora para sienpre, protesto, revoco, anulo, contradigo todo lo que en contrario pasare, dixere por qualquiera sotileza que por mi coraçón e entendimiento pasare. E quando assí fuere, atribúyolo a mi flaqueza e anduçimiento[508] del enemigo. E sojúdgome[509] a la corepçión[510] de la madre santa Iglesia commo verdadera christiana.

Oración del ángel propio. Angele Dei qui meus es custos, pietaten[511] superna me tibi comissam salva,[512] defende, guberna, illumina, benedic, santifica et ad omne bonum semper ecita.[513]

Estos quinze gozos de la gloriosa virgen santa María son por el

---

[506] *venino*: *veneno*.

[507] *quatorze artículos*: a reference to articles of faith or revealed doctrines found in the Church's creeds, organized by St. Thomas Aquinas and other medieval theologians into two sets, each of seven articles. One set deals with the majesty of divinity and the other with the mystery of the humanity of Christ.

[508] *anduçimiento*: *inducimiento*, "advice, persuasion."

[509] *sojúdgome*: ant. *sujetarse*, "to submit to the control, to be obedient."

[510] *corepçión*: *corrección*.

[511] *pietaten*: *n* lightly crossed out.

[512] *salva*: + *serva* in the margin.

[513] *ecita*: *x* added above *ec*.

número de las quinze gradas que Nuestra Señora subió[514] en el tenplo, que sinificaron[515] los mesmos [75v] gozos.[516] E ordenólos la dicha soror por aver la Virgen por abogada.

El primero. Señora santa María, madre de Dios, reina de los ángeles, abogada de los peccadores, misericordia te demando por el muy grant gozo que tú reçebiste quando el verbo de Dios desçendió del cielo, e seençeró en tus santas entrañas, e dellas tomó vestidura de omne en su propia virtud por salvar a nos. Señora María, por este primero gozo, te suplico que tú le ruegues que por tu amor él ordene mi vida, mis obras e mi fin a serviçio suyo e a salvaçión mía.

Segundo. Señora María, te demando por el gozo que tú reçebiste en nueve meses que truxiste el Fijo de Dios ençerado en el sagrario del tu vientre [76r] sin ninguna pena.

Terçero. Señora María, te demando por el gran gozo e dulçor con que el Fijo de Dios pariste.

Quarto. Señora María, te demando por el gozo que tú reçebiste quando el Fijo de Dios viste delante ti noster manificus en forma de su siervo, proçedente del tálamo de tus entrañas en su propia virtud, Dios e omne, vestido de tu carne, fermoso sobre todos fijos de Adam. E tú lo adoraste por tu verdadero Dios con gran fe, reverençia e devoçión.

Quinto. Señora María, te demando por el gozo que tú reçebiste veiéndote ser madre de Dios e omne, virgen madre parida e sin dolor.

VI. Señora María, te demando por el gozo que tú reçebiste con los ángeles que vinieron adorar [76v] el tu fijo, e con la leche que fallaste en tus pechos, ministrada de Spíritu Sancto, con que criaste al tu criador.

VII. Señora María, te demando por el gozo que tú reçebiste con el Fijo de Dios, tratándole en forma de chiquito, enbolviéndole,

---

[514] *subió*: *o* added interlinear.

[515] *sinificaron*: *significaron*, "represented."

[516] The number of joys, often five or seven, was symbolic and could include up to twenty-five. The fifteen included here derive from the *Golden Legend*, which relates that Mary, as a young child, was left to climb the fifteen steps to the temple where she remained with the other virgins.

faxándole,[517] mamantándole, falagándole,[518] arrullándole, besándole commo verdadera madre.

Ocho. Señora María, te demando por el gozo que tú reçebiste con tres reyes magos que vinieron con grande fe de lueñes[519] tierras buscando el tu fijo, Dios e omne, para lo adorar e ofrecer.

Nueve. Señora María, te demando por el gozo que tú reçebiste con tu fijo, Dios e omne, quando lo fallaste en el templo después de tres días que lo avías perdido. E tú lo buscavas [77r] con infinito trabajo e dolor.

Diez. Señora María, te demando por el gozo que tú reçebiste con tu fijo, Dios e omne, quando bolvió a ti del desierto despu[é]s de quarenta días e noches que ayunó e vençió las tentaçiones del enemigo.

XI. Señora María, te demando por los multiplicados gozos que tú reçebiste con el Fijo de Dios en este mundo, continuando su conpañía treinta e tres años, conversando, fablando con él e oyendo su santa dotrina, e veiendo las virtuosas obras que obrava, ansí commo poderoso Dios. E con pura humildat estovo a tu ordenança e mandamiento commo verdadero fijo tuyo.

XII. Señora María, te demando por el gozo que tú reçebiste la ora quel tu fijo te apareçió, Dios [77v] e omne, reçuçitado en su propia virtud fecho entre los muertos libre, te visitó e consoló con amor.

XIII. Señora María, te demando por el gozo que tú reçebiste quando el tu fijo viste sobir a los çielos en su propia virtud, Dios e omne, vestido en la carne misma que de ti tomó.

XIIII. Señora María, te demando por el gozo que tú recebiste con el Spíritu Santo quando vino sobre ti e a los apóstoles en figura de lenguas de fuego.

Quinze. Señora María, te demando por el muy conplido e acabado gozo que tú reçebiste la hora que en cuerpo e en ánima fueste sobida a los çielos e ensalçada sobre los coros de los ángeles, asentada a la diestra de Dios Padre que te crió, con el qual bives e reinas por sienpre.

Suplicaçión. [78r] Señora, yo Costança, indigna esclava tuya, que estos quinze gozos rezo, te pido merçed por reverençia dellos ayas

---

[517] *faxándole*: *fajándole*, "swaddling, wrapping."
[518] *falagándole*: *halagándole*, "caressing."
[519] *lueñes*: ant. "far, distant."

84

misericordia de mí en todas mis tribulaçiones, angustias, nescesidades. Non me desmanpares,[520] nin aborescas, nin menospreçies. Por tu virtud, miénbrate que por los pecados nasçió mi redemptor de tus entrañas. Por esta exelençia a ti dada, te suplico a la ora de mi muerte quieras ser p[   ]a[521] e defensora mía, e me libres de mis e[ne]migos e de sus tentaciones e del su poder, e me des graçia et virtud de firme fe e esperança en las llagas e muerte de mi Señor Ihesu Christo por que mi ánima se parta de mí en paz.

Protestaçión. Otrosí, muy begnigna[522] Señora, suplico a la tu magnanimidat que amanses el poderoso juez mío, [78v] tu fijo, e le ruegues que por tu amor él non me judgue en justiçia nin se mienbre de las mis eniquidades e de los grandes debdos que le yo devo; mediantes los tus mereçimientos, por exçelençia e virtud de los dolores redemptivos, plagas e muerte que por mí reçibió, le plega perdonarme mis peccados e se me muestre Dios e omne piadoso aunque soy mucho peccadora. Dios e omne lo creo; Dios e omne lo confiesso; Dios e omne lo afirmo. Protesto, revoco, anullo toda palabra o pensamiento o imaginación que en contrario dixere, lo qual atribuyo a mi flaqueza o induçimiento del enemigo. E sojúdgome a la corepçion de la madre santa Iglesia segunnt verdadera christiana.

Las siete angustias de Nuestra Señora la Virgen María. Ordenólas la dicha soror.

Bendicho sea tu coraçón, Señora, que sufrió pena en la circuncisión de tu fijo Ihesu.[523] [79r] Bendicho sea tu coraçón, Señora, que fue turvado quando oíste la prophezía del patriarca Semeón.[524] **II**.

---

[520] *desmanpares*: ant. *desampares*.
[521] The letters *p*, *n*, and *t* are visible. There is a suppression mark representing an *a* over the *t*.
[522] *begnigna*: *benigna*.
[523] This sorrow is not numbered and the last line is written below the text block. In the chronology of Luke's narrative, it does occur first (Luke 2:21).
[524] This sorrow was intended to be the first, as it begins with a larger, more ornate capital *B*. Simeon's prophecy is in Luke 2:34-35 and refers to a sword piercing Mary's heart.

Bendicho sea tu coraçón, Señora, que ovo turbaçión en la muerte de los inoçentes. E por temor de Erodes[525] levaste tu fijo a Egipto. **Tercero.** Bendicho sea tu coraçón, Señora, que tan grant dolor e vasca sufrió tres días que buscaste a tu fijo en Jherusalém. Bendicho sea tu coraçón, Señora, que padeçió soledat, estando apartada de la presencia del tu fijo quarenta días e noches quél ayunó en el desierto.[526] **IIII.** Bendicho sea tu coraçón, Señora, que fue traspasado con dolor quando oíste quel tu fijo era preso, escupido, ferido, açotado, espinado, condempnado[527] a muerte de cruz, e la viste puesta sobre sus onbros. **Quinto.** Bendicho sea tu coraçón, Señora, que fue rasgado al pie de la cruz quando viste al tu fijo enclavado, colgado en el madero, escarneçido, blasfemado, llagado, ensangustiado. Te dixo: "Mulier, [79v] ecce filius tuus." Bendicho sea tu coraçón, Señora, que fue lleno de dolor quando toviste al tu fijo en tus braços, muerto e lançeado. Bendicho sea tu coraçón, Señora, que padesçió grant dolor quando te despediste del sepulcro de tu fijo, nuestro Salvador.

Señora, yo Costança, indigna sierva tuya que estos nueve[528] graves dolores tuyos rezo con la devoçión que puedo, suplico a la tu misericordia, por reverençia dellos quieras oyr mis oraçiones, e me libres de los peligros desta vida, spirituales e corporales,[529] por que por tus merecimientos yo goze de tus gozos, donde por sienpre reynas con Dios, amén.

---

[525] *Erodes*: *h* added above the beginning of the word.
[526] This sorrow is written at the bottom of the page and extends below the text block. A symbol indicates that it is to be inserted here.
[527] *condempnado*: *condenado*.
[528] *nueve*: it appears that a previous word, perhaps *siete*, was removed and *nueve* squeezed into the space. The section title indicates seven sorrows, but there are nine sections beginning with *Bendicho sea . . . .* The two sorrows written at the bottom of folios 78v and 79r are not usually included in the traditional seven sorrows.
[529] *corporales*: + an illegible word of 3-4 letters in the margin.

86

Esta letanía que se sigue ordenó la sobredicha soror.[530]

Kyrie eleison. Christe eleison. Christe, audi nos.
[80r] Pater de celis Deus.   m
Fili Redemptor mundi Deus.   m
Spiritus Sancte Deus.   m
Sancta Trinitas unus Deus.   m

Sancta et super santissima virgo Maria, ora pro.
Mater Dei, ora pro me, Domina.
Mater fili Dei   o'
Mater verbi Dei.   o'
Mater unigeniti Dei.   o'
Mater Ihesu.   o'
Mater Christi.   o'
Filia Dei Patris.   o'
Mater filii sui.   o'
Sponsa Spiritus Sancti.   o'
Mater Dei omnipotentis.   o'
Mater Dei eterni.   o'
Mater Dei inmortalis.   o'
Mater Dei invisibilis.   o'
Mater nostri Salvatoris.   o'
Mater nostri Redemptoris.   o'
Mater nostri Creatoris.   o'
Mater nostri remisionis.   o'
[80v] Mater nostre defensionis.   o'
Mater nostre consolaçionis.   o'
Mater nostri refugii.   o'
Mater nostri toçius auxilii.   o'

[530] This litany of the Blessed Virgin Mary follows the standard form, beginning with *Kyrie* and ending with *Agnus Dei*. The first five petitions are standard, but many of the rest appear to be original. The letters at the end of the lines mean respectively: *m*: *miserere mei*; *o*: *ora pro me, Domina*; *ad*: *adjuva me*; *L*: *libera me*. In most litanies, *nobis* would be used in place of *me*.

Mater nostre fidei.	o'
Mater nostre spei.	o'
Mater nostre glorie.	o'
Mater gratie.	o'
Mater misericordie.	o'
Mater clemencie.	o'
Mater obediençie.	o'
Mater paçiençie.	o'
Mater humilitatis.	o'
Mater toçius perfectionis.	o'
Mater Dei et genitrix.	o'
Templum Domini.	o'
Sacrarium filii Dei.	o'
Tabernaclum Spiritus Sancti.	o'
Mater inmaculata.	o'
Mater intacta.	o'
Mater inviolata.	o'
Mater incontaminata.	o'

[81r] Mater et virgo perpetua. o'

Mater benedicta. o'

Mater et domina omnium virginum.

Fons pietatis.	o'
Mare magnum nostre.	o'
Spes peccatorum.	o'
Salus infirmorum.	o'
Vita mortuorum.	o'
Lux cecorum.	o'
Liberatrix captivorum.	o'

Liberatrix omnium temptaçionum demonium.

Reparatrix omnium erancium.[531] o'

Sublevatrix omnium candencium.[532] o'

---

[531] *erancium*: additional *r* interlinear, i.e., *errantium*.

[532] *candencium*: first *n* crossed out.

88

O regina et inperatrix celorum.   o'
O domina angelorum.   o'
O advocata[533] peccatorum.   o'
O mater horphanorum.[534]   o'
O mater pupilorum.   o'
O mater miserorum.   o'
O consolacio desolatorum.   o'
O via erancium.   o'
O Christianitatis remedium.   o'

[81v] Per filium tuum, adiuva me, Domina.
       Per incarnacionem eius.   ad
       Per visçera quibus filium Dei novem mensibus contulisti.   ad
       Per nativitaten eius.   ad
       Per lac uberis tui lactantis filium Dei, adiuva me, Domina.
       Per precepe[535] eius, adiuva me, Domina.
       Per circuncissionem eius.   ad
       Per bautismum eius.   ad
       Per jejunium eius.   ad
       Per orationem et sudorem sanguinis eius.   ad
       Per dura flagella que filius tuus pasus est.
       Per coronam et oprobium[536] eius.   ad
       Per admirabilem virtutem clavorum qui filii tui manus et
          pedes tranfixerunt.[537]   ad
       Per quinque plagas et crucem eius
       Per dolorem tocius corporis eius.   ad
       Per mortem et passionem eius.   ad
       Per sepulcrum eius.   ad
       Per gloriosam resureccionem eius.   ad

---

[533] *advocata*: *ca* added interlinear.
[534] *horphanorum*: second *h* added interlinear.
[535] *precepe*: *s* written over *c*.
[536] *oprobium*: read *oprobrium*.
[537] *tranfixerunt*: read *transfixerunt*.

	Per admirabilem accensionem⁵³⁸ eius.	ad
[82r]	Per Spiritum Sanctum Paraclitum.⁵³⁹	ad
	Per excelentem asumpcionem tuam.	ad

Ab omni malo libera me, Domina.
A çecitate cordis,⁵⁴⁰ ab inmundis cogitacionibus.
Ab omni inquinamento carnis et sensus mei.
Ab ira et hodio et omni mala voluntate.
A.⁵⁴¹

A malis operibus.	L
A cogitatu maligno.	L
A spiritu blasfemie.	L
Ab omni peccato desperacionis.	L
A peccati persumpcione.	L
A peccato ypocresis.	L
Ab omni peccato qui comititur contra Spiritum Sanctum.	
A pondere omni pecatorum.	L
Ab ira tua et filii tui.	L
A morte subitanea.	L
A crucitatu inferni.	L

In ora mortis mee sucure,⁵⁴² Domina.	L
In die iudicii succurre michi, Domina.	L
Ut me exaudire digneris rogo te, Domina.	

Agnus Dei, qui natus es de virgine [82v] Maria, miserere michi.
Agnus Dei, qui natus es de virgine Maria, miserere michi.
Agnus Dei, qui natus es de virgine Maria, redemptor noster, dona michi pacem.

---

⁵³⁸ *accensionem*: *s* written over first *c*.
⁵³⁹ *Per sanctam concepcionem tua* written in the upper margin, followed by *Per gloriosam natibitatem* (?) which is to be inserted on the line after *Per Spiritum . . . .* Both notes are in a different hand.
⁵⁴⁰ Vertical lines added after *cordis* to separate this line into two petitions.
⁵⁴¹ The remainder of the line is filled with a decorative rectangle.
⁵⁴² *sucure*: + *michi* interlinear.

Señor, yo Costança, tu esclava, conosco que mi sinpleza es grande.[543] E la grosería mía es fuerte porque confiesso ser mucho morante[544] e sin virtud. Creo mis obras ser defectuosas. Omilmente suplico a la tu clemençia que si en lo que yo he conpuesto, escripto en este libro, así de la oraçión de tu vida e passión, commo en las oras de los clavos, commo en la ordenaçión de las oras de la tu encarnaçión, commo en los quinze gozos e siete angustias e letanía de Nuestra Señora, que tú, Señor, non acates salvo mi deseo que fue de te loar e servir. Yo confiesso que mi entendimiento non es elevado para lo especular, nin [83r] mi coraçón capaz para lo retener, nin mi lengua es digna para lo pronunçiar por el mi grand defecto. Por ende, Señor, si alguna razón o palabra puse non bien dicha o en qualquiera manera yo erré, yo lo atribuyo a la ynorançia e ynadvertençia que en mí tiene grannt logar. Pero si así es, lo qual al presente non viene a mi notiçia, que alguna cosa menos de bien dixese, yo, asy commo fiel e católica, de agora para sienpre lo revoco e lo anulo. E sométome a la corepçión de la santa Iglesia. E suplico a ti, en cuya memoria de tu encarnaçión e pasión yo conpuse las cosas sobredichas, que me faga parçionera[545] en los méritos de las personas que lo rezaren, por que en este mundo de todos seas alabado e en el otro seamos consolados con la gloriosa visión tuya, amén

[83v] O bone Ihesu. O piissime Ihesu. O dulcissime Ihesu. O Ihesu, filii Marie, plenus misericordia et pietate. O dulçis Ihesu, secundum magnam misericordiam tuam miserere mei. O clementissime Ihesu, te deprecor per illum sanguinem preciosum quam per pecatoribus efundere voluisti ut abluas omnes iniquitates meas, et in me respiçias humiliter[546] peccatriçem et hoc nomen sanctum tuum invocantem, nomen Ihesu, nomen dulçe Ihesu.[547] Nomen delectabile. Nomen Ihesu. Nomen

---

[543] A litany is often followed by a brief prayer, in contrast to the more extensive one here which includes a supplication, a summary of the contents, and a protestation.

[544] *morante*: "lazy."

[545] *parçionera*: *partícipe*.

[546] *humiliter*: read *humilem*.

[547] *Ihesu* in the margin.

conffortans. Quid est Ihesus nisi salvator? O Ihesu, propter nomen sanctum tuum salva me ne peream, quia plassmasti me, et redemisti me, nec permitas me dapnari quem tu ex nichil[548] creasti. O bone Ihesu, ne perdat iniquitas mea quam fecit omnipotens bonitas tua. O bone Ihesu, recognosce quod tuum est et absterge quod alienum est. O Ihesu benignissime, miserere mei et dum tenpus est miserendi ne dapnes me in tenpo/re [84r] iudicandi. Que utilitas est in sanguine[549] dum desçendero in eternam corrupçionem?[550] Nec mortui laudabunt te Domine Ihesu, nec omnes qui descendunt in infernum.[551] O amantissime Ihesu. O dulcissime Ihesu. O Ihesu, Ihesu, admictere me dignare inter numerum electorum tuorum. O Ihesu, Ihesu, salus in te sperançium. O Ihesu, salus in te credencium. O Ihesu, solacium ad te confugiencium. O Ihesu, dulcis remissio omnium peccatorum. O Ihesu, filii Marie virginis, infunde in me graciam, fidem, spem et caritatem, obedienciam, paupertatem voluntariam, castitatem perpetuam, humilitatem, pacienciam et veritatem et sapienciam ut te posim perfecte diligere et cognoscere et in te gloriari.

P. Quicumque[552] vult salvus esse, ante omnia opus est ut teneat catolicam fidem, quam nisi quisque integram inviolatanque servaverit, absque [84v] dubio in eternum peribit. Fides atem catolica hec est: ut unum Deum in Trinitate et Trinitatem[553] veneremur, neque confundentes personas neque substanciam separantes. Alia est enim persona Patris,

---

[548] *nichil*: *o* added above the line after *l*.

[549] *sanguine*: + *meo* in the top margin.

[550] *Que . . . corrupçionem?*: Psalm 29:10.

[551] *Nec mortui . . . infernum*: Psalm 113:25.

[552] An exact rendering of the Athanasian Creed, also known as the *Quicunque vult*, extends to the Davidic Psalm on 86r. This creed, perhaps written in the fourth century, was in response to controversies over the person of Jesus, especially the incarnation and the relationship between Jesus's human and divine natures. Of the two main parts, the first deals with the doctrine of the Trinity and the second with the doctrine of the incarnation and redemption. In the thirteenth century, Western theologians gave this creed the same authority as the Apostles' and Nicene creeds.

[553] *Trinitatem*: + *in unitate* in the margin.

alia Filii, alia Spiritus Sancti. Set Patris et Filii et Spiritus Sancti una est divinitas, equalis gloria, coeterna magestas. Qualis Pater, talis Filius, talis Spiritus Santus. Increatus Pater, increatus Filius, increatus Spiritus Santus. Inmensus Pater, inmensus Filius, inmensus Spiritus Sanctus. Eternus Pater, eternus Filius, eternus Spiritus Sanctus. Et tamen non tres eterni, set unus eternus. Sicut non tres increati, nec tres inmensi, set unus increatus et unus inmensus. Similiter omnipotens Pater, omnipotens Filius, omnipotens Spiritus Santus. Et tamen non tres omnipotentes, set unus omnipotens. Ita Deus Pater, Deus Filius, Deus Spiritus Sanctus. Et tamen non tres [85r] dii, sed unus est Deus. Ita Dominus Pater, Dominus Filius, Dominus Spiritus Sanctus, et tamen non tres domini sed unus est Dominus. Quia sicut singillatin unamquamque personam Deum aut Dominum confiteri christiana veritate conpellimur. Ita tres deus[554] aut dominos dicere catolica religione proibemur. Pater a nullo est factus, nec creatus, nec genitus. Filius a Patre solo est: non factus, nec creatus, set genitus. Spiritus Sanctus a Patre et Filio: non factus, nec creatus, nec genitus, sed proçedens. Unus ergo Pater, non tres Patres; unus Filius, [non] tres Filii; unus Spiritus Sanctus, non tres Spiritus Sancti. Et in hac Trinitate nichil prius aut posterius, nichil manus[555] aut minus, set tote tres persone coeterne sibi sunt et coequales. Ita ut per omnia sicut iam supra dictum est, et Unitas in Trinitate, et Trinitas in Unitate, veneranda sit. Qui vult[556] ergo salvus esse, ita de [85v] Trinitate senciat.

Set necessarium est ad eternum[557] salutem ut incarnacionem quoque Domini nostri Ihesu Christi fideliter credat. Est ergo fides recta, ut credamus et confiteamur, quia Dominus noster Ihesus Christus, Dei Filius, Deus et homo est; Deus est ex substançia Patris, ante secula genitus; et homo est ex substancia matis,[558] in seculo natus. Perfectus Deus, perfectus homo ex anima racionali et humana carne subsistens,

---

[554] *deus*: read *deos*.
[555] *manus*: read *maius*, from *magnus*.
[556] *vult*: *t* added interlinear.
[557] *eternum*: read *eternam*.
[558] *matis*: read *matris*.

equalis Patri secundum divinitatem, minor Patre secundum humanitatem. Qui licet Deus sit et homo, non duo tamen, set unus est Christus; unus autem, non conversione divinitatis in carnem, set assumpcione humanitatis in Deum. Unus om[n]ino, non confusione substancie, set unitate persone. Nam sicut anima racionalis et caro unus est homo, ita Deus et homo unus est Christus. Qui passus est pro salute nostra, descendit ad inferos, [86r] tercia die resurexit a mortuis. Ascendit ad celos, sedet ad dexteram Dei Patris omnipotentis; inde venturus est iudicare vivos et mortuos. Ad cuius adventum omnes homines resurgere habent cum corporibus suis, et reddituri sunt de factis propriis racionem. Et qui bona egerunt, ibunt in vitam eternam; qui vero mala, in ignem eternum. Hec est fides catolica, quam nisi quisque fideliter firmiterque credidit, salus[559] esse non poterit.

Psalmus David.[560] Deus, Deus meus, respice in me, quare me dereliquisti? Longe a salute mea verba delictorum meorum. Deus meus, clamabo per diem et non exaudies, et nocte, non ad insipenciam michi. Tu autem in sancto habitas, laus Israel. In te speraverunt patres nostri, speraverunt et liberasti eos. At te clamaverent[561] et salvi facti sunt, in te speraverunt et non sunt confusi. Ego autem [86v] sum verimis[562] et non homo, oprobium hominum et abieccio plebis. Omnes videntes me deriserunt; me loquti sunt labiis et moverent[563] capud. Speravit in Domino; eripiat eum, salvum[564] eum quoniam[565] vult eum. Quoniam tu[566] extraxisti me de ventre, spes mea ab uberibus matris mee. In te proiectus sum ex utero. De ventre matris mee Deus meus es tu. Ne diceris[567] a me quoniam tribulacio proxima est, quoniam non est qui adiuvet.

---

[559] *salus*: read *salvus*.
[560] Psalm 21 used at Matins on Good Friday.
[561] *clamaverent*: read *clamaverunt*.
[562] *verimis*: read *vermis*.
[563] *moverent*: read *moverunt*.
[564] *salvum*: + *faciat* in the margin.
[565] *quoniam*: illegible word written interlinear + abbreviation for *quoniam* in the margin.
[566] *tu*: + *es qui* interlinear.
[567] *diceris*: read *discesseris*.

Circundederunt me vituli multi; tauri pingues obsederunt me. Ape-
ruerunt super me os suum sicut leo rapiens et rugiens. Sicut aqua
effusus sum et dispersa sunt omnia ossa mea. Factum est cor meum
tanquam cera liquecens in medio ventis[568] mei. Aruit tanquam testa
virtus mea et lingua mea adhesit faucibus meis et in pulverent[569] mortis
deduxisti me. Quoniam circundederunt me canes multi; consilium [87r]
malignançium obsedit me. Foderunt manus meas et pedes meos;
dinumeraverunt omnia ossa mea. Ipsi vero consideraverunt et
inspexerunt me; diviserunt sibi vestimenta mea et super vestem meam
miserunt sortem. Tu autem, Domine, ne[570] elongaveris auxilium tuum
a me, ad defensionem meam conspice. Erue a framea, Deus, animam
meam et de manu canis unicam meam. Salva me ex ore leonis et a
cornibus unicornium humilitatem meam. Narabo nomen tuum fratribus
meis; in medio ecclesie[571] laudabo te. Qui timetis Dominum, laudate
eum; universum semen Iacob, glorificate eum. Timeat eum omne semen
Israel quoniam non sprevit neque despexit deprecacionem pauperis. Nec
avertit faciem suam a me et cum clamarem ad eum exaudivit me. Apud
te laus mea in ecclesia magna, vota mea reddam in cospectu[572]
timen/cium [87v] eum. Edent pauperes et saturabuntur, et laudabunt
Dominum qui requirunt eum; vivent corda eorum in seculum seculi.
Reminiscentur et convertentur ad Dominum universi fines terre. Et
adorabunt in conspectu eius universe familie gencium. Quoniam Domini
est regnum et ipse dominabitur gencium. Manducaverunt et adoraverunt
omnes pingues terre; in conspectu eius cadent omnes qui descendunt in
teram. Et anima mea illi vivet, et semem meum serviet ipsi.
Anunciabitur Domino generatio ventura, et anunciabunt celi iusticiam
eius populo qui nascetur: quem fecit Dominus.

---

[568] *ventis*: read *ventris*.
[569] *pulverent*: read *pulverem*.
[570] *ne*: *nec*: with *c* crossed out.
[571] *ecclesie*: + two letters (? *ce*) crossed out.
[572] *cospectu*: *conspectu*.

Prosa.[573] Veni, Sancte Spiritus, et emite celitus lucis tue radium. Veni, pauperum Pater; veni, dator munerum; veni, lumen cordium. Consolator optime, dulcis ospes anime, dulce refrigerium. In labore requies, in estu temperies, in flectu solacium. O lux beatissima, reple cordis intima tuorum [88r] fidelium; sine tuo numine nichil est in homine, nichil est innoxium. Lava quod est sordidum, riga quod est aridum. Sana quod est saucium. Flecte quod est rigindum,[574] fove quod est frigidum, rege quod est devium. Da tuis fidelibus in te confidentibus sacrum septenarium. Da virtutis meritum. Da salutis exitum. Da perempne gaudium. **Antiphana**. Veni, Sancte Spiritus, reple tuorum corda fidelium et tui amoris in eis ignem ascende, qui per diversitatem multarum lingarum gentes in unitate fidei congregasti, aleluya. ℞. Emitte Spiritum tuum et creabuntur. ℣. Et renovabis faciem terre.

Oraçión. Deus qui corda fidelium Sancti Spiritus illustracione docuisti, da nobis in eodem Spiritu recta sapere, et de eius semper consolacione gaudere. Per eiusdem.

Manificat anima mea Dominum.[575] Et exultavit spiritus meus in Deo salutari meo. Quia respexit humilitaten ancille sue, ecce enim ex [88v] hoc beata[576] me dicent omnes generaciones. Quia fecit michi malriia[577] qui potens est, et sanctum nomen eius, et misericordia eius a progenie et in progenies timentibus eum. Fecit potenciam in brachio suo, dispersit superbos mente cordis sui. Deposuit potentes de sede et exaltavit humiles. Exurientes inplevit bonis et divites dimissit inanes. Suscepit Israel puerum suum, recordatus misericordie sue, sicut locutus est ad patres nostros, Abraham et semini eius in secula. Gloria Patri et Filio.

---

[573] This paragraph and the following prayer are the same Pentecost sequence as above on 30v-31r.

[574] *rigindum*: *rigidum*.

[575] A red *c* after *Dominum*. The *Magnificat*, Luke 1:46-55, is sung each night at Vespers.

[576] *beata*: read *beatam*.

[577] *malriia*: or *malrna*? The reading is not clear, as the *r* is darker and may have been written over previous letters. The Vulgate reads *magna*.

Antiphana.[578] Ave, stella matutina, peccatorum medicina, mundi princeps et regina, sola virgo digna dici, contra tella inimici clipeum pone salutis tue titulum virtutis. O sponsa Dei electa, esto nobis via recta ad eterna gaudia. Ora pro nobis, sancta Dei genitrix. ℞. Set digni efficiamur promisionibus Christi.

Oración. Graciam tuam, quesumus, Domine, mentibus [89r] nostris infunde ut qui, Angelo nunciante, Christi Filii tui incarnacionem cognovimus, per passionem eius et crucem ad resurrectionis gloriam perducamur, per eumdem.

Psalmus Davit.[579] Misericordias Domini in eternum cantabo. In generacione[580] et generacionem anunciabo veritatem tuam in ore meo. Quoniam dixisti: In eternum misericordia hedificabitur in celis, preparabitur veritas tua in eis. Disposui testamentum electis meis, iuravi David, servo meo: usque in eternum preparabo semen tuum, et hedificabo in generacione et generacionem sedem tuam. Confitebuntur celi mirabilia tua, Domine, etenim veritatem tuam in ecclesia sanctorum. Quoniam quis in nobibus[581] equabitur Domino, aut quis similis erit Deo in filiis Dei? Deus qui glorificatur in consilio sanctorum, magnus et terribilis super [89v] omnes qui in circuitu eius sunt. Domine Deus virtutum, quis similis tibi? Potens es, Domine, et veritas tua in circuitu tuo. Tu dominaris potestati maris, motum autem fluctum eius tu mitigas. Tu humiliasti sicut vulneratum superbum, in brachio virtutis tue dispersisti inimicos tuos. Tui sunt celi, et tua est terra; orbem terre et plenitudinem eius tu fundasti; aquilonem et mare tu creasti. Tabor et Hermon in nomine tuo exultabunt, tuum brachium cum potencia, firmetur manus tua et exaltetur dextera tua, iusticia et iudicium preparacio sedis tue. Misericordia et veritas precedem[582] faciem tuam. Beatus populus qui scit iubilacionem. Domine, in lumine vultus tui

---

[578] Antiphon used at Lauds in the Saturday Office of the Blessed Virgin Mary, followed by the prayer used at Prime in the Little Office of the BVM.

[579] Psalm 88 used at Matins on Fridays and Christmas.

[580] *generacione*: read *generacionem*.

[581] *nobibus*: *nubibus*.

[582] *precedem*: *precedent*.

ambulabunt, et in nomine tuo exultabunt tota die, et in iusticia tua exaltabuntur. Quoniam gloria virtutis eorum tu es, et in bene/placito [90r] tuo exaltabitur cornu nostrum. Quia Domini est assunpcio[583] nostra et sancti Israel regis nostri. Tunc locutus es in visione sanctis tuis et dixisti: Posui adiutorium [in] potente, et exaltavi[584] electum de plebe mea. Inveni David, servum[585] meum, oleo sancto meo unxi exum.[586] Manus enim mea auxiliabitur ei et brachium meum confortavit eum. Nichil proficiet inimicus in eo et filius iniquitatis non aponet nocere ei. Et concidam a facie ipsius inimicos eius, et odientes eum in fugam convertam. Et veritas mea et misericordia mea cum ipso, et in nomine meo exaltabitur cornu eius. Et ponam in mari manum eius, et in fluminibus dexteram eius. Ipse invocavit me: Pater meus es tu, Deus meus, et susceptor salutis mee. Et ego primogenitum ponam illum, excelsum pre regibus terre. In eternum servabo illi [90v] misericordiam mean[587] et testamentum meum fidele ipsi. Et ponam in seculum seculi semen eius, thronum eius sicut dies celi. Si autem derelinquerunt[588] filii eius legem meam et in iudiciis meis non anbulaverint, si iusticias mea[589] prophanaverint et mandata mea non custodiri[n]t, visitabo in virga iniquitates eorum et in verberibus peccata eorum. Misericordiam autem meam non disperdam[590] ab eo neque nocebo ei[591] in veritate mea. Neque prophanabo testamentum meum, et que procedunt de labiis meis non faciam irrita. Semel iuravi in sancto meo si David menciar, semen eius in eternum manebit. Et thronus eius sic[592] sol in co[n]spectu meo et sicut luna perfecta [in] eternum et testis in celo fidelis. Tu vero repulisti et

---

[583] *assunpcio*: i.e., *assumptio*.
[584] *exaltavi*: final *t* scraped off.
[585] *servum*: + *me*.
[586] *exum*: read *eum*.
[587] *mean*: *meam*.
[588] *derelinquerunt*: read *dereliquerint*.
[589] *mea*: changed to *mia*, read *meas*.
[590] *disperdam*: read *dispergam*.
[591] *ei*: crossed out.
[592] *sic*: read *sicut*.

98

despexisti et⁵⁹³ distulisti christum tuum. Avertisti⁵⁹⁴ testamentum servi tui, prophanasti in tera sanctuarium Dei,⁵⁹⁵ destruxisti omnes sepes eius, posuisti firma/mentum [91r] eius formidinem. Diripuerunt eum omnes transeuntes viam, factus est obprobium vicinis suis. Exaltasti dexteram deprimencium eum, letificasti omnes inimicos eius. Avertisti adiutorium gladii eius et non ex⁵⁹⁶ auxiliatus ei in bello. Destruxisti eum ab emundacione et sedem eius in terra collisti.⁵⁹⁷ Minorasti dies temporis eius, perfudisti eum confusione. Usquequo, Domine, avertis in finem, exardescet sicut ignis ira tua? Memorare que mea substancia, numquid enim vane constituisti omnes filios hominum? Quis est homo qui vivet et non videbit mortem, eruet animam suam de manu inferi? Ubi sunt misericordie tue antique, Deo,⁵⁹⁸ sicut iurasti David in veritate tua? Memor esto, Domine, obprobii servorum tuorum, quod continui in sinu meo multarum gencium. Quod exprovaverunt⁵⁹⁹ inimici tui, Domine, quod exprovaverunt comutacionem christi tui. Benedictus Dominus Deus in eternum.⁶⁰⁰

[91v] Clementissime Domine Ihesu, ipse Fili Dei vivi qui non vis mortem peccatorum, nec delectaris in perdicione moriencium, scis quod lacrime, quod suspiria, quid⁶⁰¹ gemitus, quid singultus⁶⁰² absymo⁶⁰³ eructus deposcat. Peccatrix sum, et inmunda et omnium nesfandorum⁶⁰⁴ labe poluta sum, ad te qui es fons misericordie curro, ut male perditam restituas, restaures et restituas vitam. Et me de tartari faucibus clementer eripias, potenter extrahaas, misericorditer eruas qui solus laborem et

---

⁵⁹³ *et*: crossed out.
⁵⁹⁴ *Avertisti*: i.e., *evertisti*.
⁵⁹⁵ *Dei*: read *eius*.
⁵⁹⁶ *ex*: read *es*.
⁵⁹⁷ *terra collisti*: read *terram collisisti*.
⁵⁹⁸ *Deo*: read *Domine*.
⁵⁹⁹ *exprovaverunt*: i.e., *exprobraverunt*.
⁶⁰⁰ *Fiat Fia[t]* added in the margin.
⁶⁰¹ *quid*: *d* very faint, possibly erased.
⁶⁰² *singultus*: *singulatus* with the *a* scratched out.
⁶⁰³ *absymo*: read *abysmo*.
⁶⁰⁴ *nesfandorum*: read *nefandorum*.

dolorem consideras. Qui vivis et regnas Deus per omnia secula seculorum. Amen.

Creo por coraçón puro, e por boca acabada confiéssolo ser verdadero Dios e omne mi Señor Ihesu Christo, fijo del Padre perdurable e de la virgen madre, precio de la redempción de la mi ánima. Vida de la mi peregrinaçión, [92r] por cuyo amor tengo la santa fe católica. Señor, por la mi flaqueza en muchas cosas e menguas te ofendí. E turbé el tu grant poderío. E tú, piadoso e misericordioso, das misericordia a todos los que llaman el tu sancto nonbre Ihesu. E por ende, mucho piadoso Señor, te ruego por tu grant miseriacordia[605] e por virtud de la tu santa passión que quieras perdonar a mí pecatriz, tu sierva. Qui cum Deo Patre in unitate.[606]

Dios te salve, preciosa carne de Ihesu Christo, la qual por mí padesciste. Dentro me alinpia, carne santa. E honda de sangre de Ihesu Christo, por ti sea alinpiado el mi seso e purificado en verdadera manera, a la qual se canta: Osana. Dame tu vida quando viniere el tienpo de la tu yra.

A ti, Señora piadosa, me encomiendo. Santa María, madre de Dios, verda/dera [92v] virgen santa sin erança,[607] sey tú mi firme esperança en el día postrimero.

Yo te adoro, verdat digna que so essa blanca figura estás ascondida.[608] El mi coraçón en ti a[609] grande affección[610] porque contenplando en ti del todo fallecçe el viso,[611] el gusto, el tacto en ti se engaña. Pero

---

[605] *miseriacordia*: read *misericordia*.

[606] A line from the Nicene Creed.

[607] *erança*: *erranza*, ant. *error, yerro*.

[608] Contemplation of the Host naturally follows Constanza's confession of belief in the divine and human natures of Christ and her references to the saving power of his body and blood. Using mystical language of adoration, she further affirms the Catholic belief in the real sacrificial presence of Christ under the eucharistic symbols and ends her prayer in anticipation of his physical presence at the end of time.

[609] *a*: read *ha*, ant. *tiene*.

[610] *affección*: the *e* was altered from an original *i*.

[611] *viso*: ant. *vista*.

por sola oyda yo en ti verdaderamente creo todas las cosas quel Fijo de Dios dixo porque non ay cosa más ver[da]dera que la su palabra. En la cruz estava ascondida sola[612] divinidat; en ti está ascondida la divinidat e la humanidat. Todo lo creo e lo confiesso, e pido lo que pidió el ladrón penitente.[613] Non veo yo las llagas commo vido santo Tomás, pero yo te confiesso ser verdadero Dios mío. Fazme sienpre creer en ti con esperança e amor. O memorial de la muerte del Señor, o pan que das vida al omne, da [93r] tú a la mi alma que biva, biva de ti. E dale en ti dulce sabor. O piadoso pelicano, Señor Ihesu Christo, alínpiame a mí por la tu preciosa sangre, el destello[614] de la qual puede a todo el mundo salvar, e a todos nos puede fazer sin peccado. O Señor Ihesu Christo, el qual agora veo velado, ¿quándo se conplirá en mí lo que agora deseo por que te yo pueda ver revelado en la gloria eternal bienaventurado? Amén.

O benignissime Ihesu Christe, respice super me, miseram peccatricem, occlis tue misericordie cum quibus respexisti Petrum, Matheum et Mariam Magdalenam in comunio[615] et latrronem in cruc[i]s[616] patibulo, et da michi pecatrici ut cum Petro mea peccata defleam et cum Maria Magdalena ut perfecte te diligam et cum latrone in celesti paradiso te videam ubi cum Patre et Spiritu Sancto regnas Deus in secula seculorum. Amen.

[93v] El papa Benifacio Sexto,[617] a petiçión de Felipo rey de Françia,

---

[612] *sola*: + *la* added interlinear.

[613] Luke 23:42: "Jesus, remember me when you come in your kingly power."

[614] *destello*: "a flowing drop by drop."

[615] *comunio*: read *communione*.

[616] *cruc[i]s*: *s* added in the margin.

[617] Pope Boniface VI died fifteen days after his election in 896. The reference may be to Boniface VIII, pope from 1294 to 1303 during the reign of Philip IV of France, although the repeated struggles between them over issues of sovereignty casts doubt on the historicity of such a petition. Similar versions of this prayer with the same dispensations occur frequently in fifteenth-century

otorgó dos mill años de perdón a qualquier que dixere esta oración yuso[618] escripta, después que fuere alçado el cuerpo de Dios fasta el terçero Agnus Dei.

Domine Ihesu Christe, qui hanc sacratissiman carnem de gloriose virginis Marie utero assumpssisti, et eundem preciosum sanguinem de santissimo latere tuo in ara crucis pro salute nostra efundisti. Et in hac gloriosa carne a mortuis resuressisti et ad celos ascendisti. Et iterum venturus est cum gloria, judicare vivos et mortuos.[619] In eadem carne libera me per hoc sacratissimum corpus tuum quomodo tactatur in alteri[620] presenti ab omnibus inmundiciis mentis et corporis, et ab universis malis, et periculis corporis et anime preteritis, presentibus et fucturis nunc et in eternum. Amen.

[94r] **Epístola de santo Ynacio.**[621] Christifere Marie, suus Ignacio salutem.[622] Me neophitum Ioanisque[623] tui discipulum confortare et consolari debueras; de Ihesu filio tuo percepi miranda dictu, et stupefactus sum ex auditu. A te autem que semper ei fuisti familiariter[624] conjunta et secretorum eius conscia, desidero[625] animo fieri cercior de auditis; scripsi tibi alias, et rogavi de eisdem. Valeas, et neophiti qui mecum[626] sunt, ex te et per te et in te confortentur. Amen.

El romançe. A María que a Christo trajo, el su Ignacio. Devieras confortar e consolar a mí, nuevo en la fe e deçiplo del tu Juan qua[627] del

---

books of hours. See, for example, BN (Madrid) MS 6539, *Libro devocionario y horas*

[618] *yuso*: ant. "below."

[619] *Et iterum . . . mortuos* is from the Nicene Creed.

[620] *alteri*: *altari*.

[621] The letters of St. Ignatius to Mary and John along with their replies belong to the apocryphal Ignatian epistles popular in the Middle Ages.

[622] *salutem*: added above the line into the margin.

[623] *Ioanisque*: *h* added above *oa*.

[624] *familiariter*: *ter* squeezed into the space.

[625] *desidero*: + *ex* interlinear.

[626] *mecum*: *c* added above.

[627] *qua*: *ca*, ant. "because."

tu Ihesu sentí cosas maravillosas de dezir e estó espavoreçido[628] del oír, mas deseo en mi coraçón ser fecho más çierto de ti que sienpre a él fuste junta, familiar e sabidora de los secretos dél de las cosas oydas. Ante escre/ví [94v] otra vez e te rogué sobre ellas. Valgas en Dios e los nuevos en la fe que comigo están, sean de ti e por ti e en ti confortados. **Epístola de Nuestra Señora a sancto Yna[cio].**[629] Ignacio, dilecto diciplo, humilis ancilla Christi Ihesu. De Ihesu que a Juane[630] audisti et didicisti, vera sunt. Illa credas, illis inhereas, et Christianitatis votum firmiter teneas, et mores et vitam voto conformes. Veniam atem una cum Iohane, te et qui tecum sunt visitare.[631] Sta et viriliter age in fide. Nec te moveat[632] persecuçionis austeritas, set valeat et exultet spiritus tuus in Deo, salutari tuo. **Romançe.** A Ignacio amado diciplo, la humil sierva de Ihesu Christo. Aquellas cosas que de Ihesu oíste e aprendiste de[633] Juan, verdaderas son. Aquellas cree e a ellas te allega. E ten firmemente el voto de la christiandat e conforma el voto, las costunbres e la vida, mas yré yo de confirmo con Juan a te ver e a los [95r] que contigo están. Sta[634] en la fe e obra virilmente; nin te mueva la aspereza de la perse-cución, mas valgas en Dios. E tu spíritu se alegre en Dios, Salvador tuyo. Así sea conplido. **Letra de sancto Inaçio a sant Juan.** Iohani santo seniori, suus Ignacius et qui cum eo sunt fratres. De tua mora dolemus graviter, allocucionibus et consolacionibus tuis roborandi. Si tua absencia protendatur multos de nostris destituet. Properes igitur venire quia cxpedire credimus. Sunt et hic multe de nostris mulieribus, Mariam Ihesum videre cupientes, et cotidie a nobis ad vos discurrere volentes, ut eam contingant et ubera eius contrattent que Dominum Ihesum aluerunt

---

[628] *espavoreçido*: *expavecido*, "struck with fear or astonishment."

[629] *Yna[cio]*: written in the margin and partially lost in the binding.

[630] *Juane*: i.e., *Johanne*.

[631] *visitare*: *sitare* squeezed into the space, in a different hand. Probably replaces *visere*.

[632] Symbol for *con* added above the beginning of *moveat*.

[633] *de*: interlinear.

[634] *Sta*: originally *santa* with *an* scraped out.

et quedam secreciora eius percuntentur. E Salome quam diligis, filia Anne Ierosolimis, quinque mensibus comorans apud eam. Et quidam noti referunt eamdem matrem Dei omnium graciarum abundantem[635] et omnium virtutum[636] fecundam. Et ut [95v] dicunt in persecucionibus et aflictionibus est ilaris, in penurio et indigenciis non querula, iniuriantibus grata et molestata letatur, miseris et aflictis condolet et subvenire non pigrescit.[637]

Romançe. A Juan santo senior. El su Ignacio e los hermanos que con él son. De tu tardança gravemente nos dolemos, aviendo de ser esforçados de[638] tus fablas[639] e consolaçiones. Si tu absençia se aproluenga,[640] muchos de nosotros destituirá.[641] Por ende apresúrate venir ca creemos convenir. E son aquí muchas de las mugeres de nosotros que cobdician[642] ver a María[643] de Ihesu. E cada día quieren discurrir de nosotros a vosotros por que tangan[644] aquella e tracten[645] las tetas de ella que al Señor Ihesu criaron e algunas cosas más secretas della pregunten. E Salomé, fija de Anna, la qual amas, que çerca della moró çinco meses en [96r] Jherusalém. Et otros conosçidos cuentan essa María, madre de Dios, ser abundosa de todas graças e pregonada de todas virtudes. E según dizen en las presecuçiones e aflicçiones es plazentera e en las menguas e menesteres non querellosa, e es grata a los que la injurian e molestada se alegra, conduélese a los míseros e aflictos e non se enpereça[646] en los subvenir. Valgas en Dios, así sea conplido.

---

[635] *abundantem*: *tem* added in the margin.
[636] *virtutum* repeated but crossed out.
[637] The last half of the Ignatian letter is omitted here.
[638] *de*: added interlinear.
[639] *fablas*: *hablas*, ant. "words spoken, exhortations."
[640] *aproluenga*: ant. *prolongar*.
[641] *destituirá*: second *i* added interlinear.
[642] *cobdician*: read *cobdician*, i.e., *codician*.
[643] *María*: + *madre* interlinear.
[644] *tangan*: ant., subjunctive of *tañer*, used with the same meaning as *tocar*.
[645] *tracten*: ant. *traten*.
[646] *enpereça*: *emperezarse*, "to let oneself be dominated by laziness."

Carta de Ignacio a sant Juan. Juani sancto seniori, suus Ignacius. Si licitum est michi apud te, ad Ierosolime partes volo ascendere, et videre fideles sanctos qui ibi sunt; precipue Mariam Ihesu, quam dicunt universi admirandam et cuntis desiderabilem. Quem[647] enim non delectet videre eam et alloqui que nostrum Deum de se peperit, si nostre sit fidei et religionis amicus? Similiter illum venerabilem Iacobum qui cogno[m]/inatur [96v] Justus, quem referunt Christo Ihesu similimum facie, et vita et modo conversaçionis, ac si eiusdem uteri frater esset gemellus. Quem si videro, videbo Ihesum secundum omnia corporis eius liniamenta. Preterea ceteros sanctos et santas.[648] Heu, quid moror? Cur detineor? Bone preceptor, properare me iubeas et valeas. Amen.

Romance. Juan sancto senior.[649] El su Ignacio. Si cerca de ti me es lícito, sobir quiero a las partes de Jerusolima e ver los fieles sanctos que ende[650] son, mayormente a María[651] de Ihesu, la qual dizen ser a todos de maravillar e [a] todos deseable. E ¿a quién non delecte[652] ver e fablar aquella que de sí a nuestro Dios parió, si de nuestra fe e nuestra religión es amigo? E[653] semejablemente ver aquel venerable Iacobo, el qual es cognominado Justo, el qual cuentan ser muy semejable a Ihesu en la faz, en vida, en manera de con/versaçión, [97r] commo si fuesse su hermano de un vientre gemello mellizos. El qual me dizen si viere esse[654] Ihesu segunt las façiones del cuerpo dél. E asimesmo ve[655] a los otros santos e santas. ¡Hay! ¿Por qué me tardo? ¿Por qué me detengo? Buen mandador, mandadme apresurar. E valgas en Dios, así cunpla.

---

[647] *Quem*: read *Quis*.
[648] *santas*: *c* added above *nt*.
[649] *viejo*: in the margin.
[650] *ende*: ant. *allí*.
[651] *María*: + *madre* in the margin.
[652] *delecte*: ant. *deleitar*.
[653] *amigo?* *E*: *co* interlinear after *amigo*. An ink blot covers *E*.
[654] *esse*: possibly a latinized form of *ser* as a verb is lacking.
[655] *ve*: final *r* scraped off.

Capítulo de las preguntas que deven fazer al omne desque está en punto de muerte[656]

Si por ventura el enfermo o enferma non están[657] dispuesta para bien morir, que sea informada de aquellas cosas que son salvaçión de su ánima. Las preguntas son éstas. Primeramente le deve preguntar: hermana, ¿plázete de morir en la fe de Ihesu Christo? Responda sí. E después dígale: hermana, ¿conosces que non as servido a Dios tan bien segunt [97v] devías? Diga sí. ¿Arepientes[658] dello? Responda sí. ¿Tienes tú voluntad de te enmendar si Dios te dier[659] espaçio[660] e vida? Responda sí. ¿Crees que por ti padesçió muerte e passión Ihesu Christo, nuestro Redemptor, Fijo de Dios? Responda sí. ¿Crees que non puedes ser salva si non por la su passión? Responda sí. Pues, hermàna, mientra en ti es el ánima, dale muchas graçias e en la su[661] sola muerte ten esperança de te salvar e non en otra cosa alguna, e a él en esta muerte te encomienda e en él pon toda tu confiança e non en otro. E si por aventura el Señor Dios te quisier judgar, di: O Señor, la muerte de mi Señor Ihesu Christo pongo entre mí e los mis malos mereçimientos e el tu juizio. En otra manera, Señor, non contiendo contigo en juizio. E si el Señor te dixere que mereçes dapnaçión, di: La muerte de mi Se/ñor [98r] Ihesu Christo pongo entre mí e los mis malos mereçimientos, e la su muy digna passión ofresco por contrición que yo pecadora devía tener e por mi culpa non lo tengo. E después diga: O Señor, la muerte del Nuestro Redemptor pongo entre mí e la tu ira. Después diga tres vezes: Señor, en las tus manos encomiendo el mi espíritu. Eso mesmo digan las que están presentes. E si por ventura la enferma non pudier fablar,

---

[656] *vaco* or *vaci*: written at the edge of the page opposite this heading. The questions to be asked in preparation for death have been attributed to St. Anselm and appear in numerous medieval codices. A similar version in Spanish is BN (Madrid) MS 6485, *Breve tratado que se llama arte de bien morir*.

[657] *están*: read *está*.

[658] *arepientes*: + *te* interlinear.

[659] *dier*: apocopated form of the future subjunctive *diere*. Compare *quisier* (97v), *pudier* (98r), etc.

[660] *espaçio*: i.e., "period of time."

[661] *su*: repeated and crossed out.

las que están presentes digan tres vezes: Señor, en llas⁶⁶² tus manos encomendamos el su spíritu. E çiertamente muere segura e non verá la muerte perpetua.

E aunque estas preguntas sobredichas se deven fazer a todas presonas, más conveniblemente se deven fazer a religiosos e a presonas devotas. Díganle: ¿Renunçias e aboreçes todas eregías e erores e falsas [98v] dotrinas reprovadas por la madre sancta Iglesia? ¿E alégraste que mueres en la fe de Ihesu Christo e unidat e obediençia de la madre sancta Iglesia? Lo segundo sea preguntada: ¿Conoçes que al tu Criador muchas vezes as ofendido, que ninguno non se puede salvar sin conosçer a sí mesmo? Lo terçero a de ser preguntado: ¿Arepiénteste en tu coraçón de todos los pecados que contra Dios, Redemptor tuyo Ihesu Christo, as cometido? ¿Arepiénteste? E eso mesmo de los bienes que pudieras fazer, porque non los feçiste e de muchos grandes e estintos⁶⁶³ de bien que menospreçiaste: ¿De todo esto te desplaze, no solamente por temor que agora as de morir, nin eso mesmo por temor de pena alguna, mas solamente por amor⁶⁶⁴ que as a Dios ofendido? Todo cristiano es obligado de amar a Dios sobre todas las cosas e de buen coraçón. [99r] ¿Demandas de todos estos pecados perdón? ¿Cobdiçias eso mesmo que tu coraçón sea alumbrado a conosçer los peccados que as cometido contra Dios por que dellos espeçialmente puedes⁶⁶⁵ aver penitencia? Dévele ser preguntado lo quarto: Hermana, ¿propones verdaderamente de te enmendar de todos estos yeros e defectos si ovieres de escapar desta enfermedat?

Oración de sancto. Otórgame, Señor,⁶⁶⁶ misericordioso Dios, aquellas cosas que a ti son placenteras: codiciar con grande ardor et verdaderamente conocer e cuerdamente las buscar et perfectamente las acabar, a loor e honrra e gloria del tu sancto nonbre. Ordena, Señor,

---

⁶⁶² *llas*: i.e., *las*.
⁶⁶³ *estintos*: ant. *instintos*.
⁶⁶⁴ *amor*: possibly should read *temor*.
⁶⁶⁵ *puedes*: read *puedas*.
⁶⁶⁶ *Señor*: crossed out in red.

el[667] mi estado e fazme saber todo aquello que tienes por bien en [99v] que te he de servir. E dame gracia que lo pueda conplir por obra, ansí commo pertenesce e cunple a la mi ánima. Señor, la carrera por que [he] de venir a ti séame segura, derecha e confirmada que non fallesca entre bienandanças e tribulaciones, mas que en los bienes te dé grandes gracias et en las tribulaciones guarde mi coraçón en paciençia verdadera por que non se levante mi coraçón en los bienes nin se abaxe en los males. De nenguna cosa non se goze si non de la que le acarea[668] a ti. E de ninguna cosa non se duela si non de la que le arriedra de ti. A ninguno non desee fazer plazer si non a ti, nin tema de fazer pesar si non a ti. Todas las cosas que han poco de durar me parescan viles por tu amor. Las tus cosas ame [100r] de coraçón e a ti más que a todas. Enojo me sea todo gozo que es sin ti. Deleite me sea todo trabajo que es por ti. Et enojosa me sea toda folgança que non es en ti. Endereça sienpre el mi coraçón a ti et fazme pensar con dolor et proposición de emienda en todas mis menguas. Dios mío, fazme omilde sin enfinta;[669] triste me faz sin caer mi coraçón; cuerdo e pesado sin graveza, ligera sin liviandat, verdadera sin dobleza, que te tema sin desperación, que espere en ti sin presunción e pueda castigar mi próximo sin simulación et edificarlo por palabra et emxenplo sin desdén de coraçón. Fazme obediente sin contradición, paciente sin murmuración. O muy dulce Dios, otórgame coraçón velador que lo non arriedre de ti vano pensamiento. Dame coraçón non mueble[670] que lo [100v] non abaxe liviano talente.[671] Dame coraçón non vencido que lo non quebrante cosa alguna endereçada a ti, que lo non buelva sinistra entinción.[672] Dame coraçón libre en que maldat ninguna non se pueda enseñorear. Otórgame, muy dulce Dios, entendimiento que te conosca. Otórgame

---

[667] *el*: crossed out in red.
[668] *acarea*: ant. *llevar, guiar*.
[669] *enfinta*: ant. *ficción, engaño, fingimiento*.
[670] *mueble*: ant. *movible, movedizo*.
[671] *talente*: ant. *talante*, "desire, will, disposition."
[672] *sinistra entinción*: *siniestra intención*.

amor e acucia[673] para te buscar. Enbíame sabiduría con que te pueda fallar, vida e conversación a ti plazentera, pensamiento que fielmente espere en ti. Enbíame fiuza[674] que a ti me llegue. Otórgame conpassión de tus penas, gracia de tus beneficios e en este mundo gloria de los tus gozos e en el otro mundo do bives e regnas para sienpre bendicho. Amén.

"Fili, quid fecisti nobis sic? Ego et pater tuus dolentes, querebamus te." Et [ait ad illos:] "Quid est quod me querebatis? Nesciebatis quia in hiis que patris mei sunt, oportet me esse?"[675]

[101r] **Suplicatio. In die mortis.**[676] Porque el término de mi vida se acaba, nescesario es dar cuenta.

Yo Constança me confieso a ti, Señor mi Dios, que soy grave peccadora, que despendí[677] toda mi vida mal obrando. Traspasé tu voluntad por conplir la mía. Arrepiéntome e pésame de quantos pecados fiz.[678] Suplico a ti, Ihesu Christo mi Señor, que me des gracia que me enmiende. Yo propongo de lo así fazer. Señor Ihesu Christo, por tu clemençia me da gracia que muera creyendo, confesando tu sancta fe conplidamente. Señor, si tu voluntad es de me levar[679] este día o noche, ofresco e pongo entre [101v] ti e mis debdas tu sancta encarnaçión e todas las penas que padesçió tu humanidat por mí, Señor, por el defecto grande que en mí es del dolor e contriçión que devía tener mirando las grandes ofensas que a ti fiz, e desconosçimiento de los muchos e grandes benefiçios que obró tu mano poderosa en mí, gusano sin provecho. A

---

[673] *e acucia*: obscured by ink blots; ant. "zeal."

[674] *fiuza*: *fiucia*, "trust, confidence."

[675] Luke 2:48-49. Used at Matins on 11 October, the Feast of the Motherhood of the Blessed Virgin Mary. The passage begins with an ornate capital and is written in a smaller script within the letter block at the end of the folio. The preceding prayer, these lines, and the following material are in three distinct hands.

[676] *Suplicatio . . . mortis*: in red in the top margin.

[677] *despendí*: "used, wasted."

[678] *fiz*: *fize, hice.*

[679] *levar*: + *desta vid[a]* in the margin.

ti mesmo, Ihesu, ofresco en pago de mis debdas[680] los crueles dolores que sufriste en la[681] cruz, estando descoiuntado e enclavado con tres clavos. Señor, miénbrate que el preçio de mi ánima es la sagrada sangre [102r] tuya que por cinco partes de tu cuerpo salió abondosa con espantosos e graves dolores, fasta que te fizieron dar el spíritu. Señor Ihesu, estos propios méritos tuyos pongo entre mí e la tu ira. En otra manera non contiendo contigo en juizio. Cierto es que meresco danaçión. Yo ansí lo creo, lo confieso, e temo. Suplico con aquella omilldat e reverençia que puedo de la sentençia que meresçen mis culpas para ti mesmo, Ihesu, redemptor mío et juez mío, mediador, Deus et homo, que me acates[682] segund la grandeza de la tu grand missericordia.

In manus tuas, [102v] Domine, comendo spiritum meum,[683] *tres vezes.* Domine Ihesu Christe, Fili Dei vivi, pone passionem et crucem et mortem[684] inter iudicium tuum et animam meam.[685]

Anima Christi, sanctifica me. Corpus Christi, salva me. Sanguis Christi, inebria me. Aqua lateris Christi, lava me. Passio Christi, conforta me. O bone Ihesu, exaudi me. Ne permitas me separari a te. Ab oste maligno defende me. In hora mortis mee voca me. Et pone me iusta[686] te ut cum angelis tuis laudem te in secula seculorum. Amen.[687]

Domine, ne in furore tuo arguas me, neque in ira tua corripias me. Miserere mei, Domine, quoniam infirma sum, sana me, Domine. Sana animam meam quia tibi soli[688]

---

[680] *debdas*: + *rigiditas [e]t dureza mía* in the margin.

[681] *la*: + red cross symbol.

[682] *acates*: + *e me judgu[es]* in the margin.

[683] *In . . . meum*: response at Compline.

[684] *mortem*: + *tuam* in the margin.

[685] *meam*: + *[n]unc et in [or]a mortis [m]ee largi[ri] digneris* in the margin.

[686] *iusta*: *iuxta.*

[687] The *Anima Christi* is listed among the prayers to be said after Mass. Of unknown authorship, it appeared as early as the fourteenth century and was included frequently in fifteenth-century devotional books.

[688] Psalm 6:1-2, used in the Office of the Dead. The last six words, not included in the psalm, form an incomplete thought, indicating the omission of a word or the loss of a folio.

110

[103r]   qui pro novis vulneratus est, o.[689]
qui pro novis flagelatus est, o.
qui pro novis coronatus est, o.
qui pro novis condenatus est, o.
qui pro novis enclavatus est, o.
qui pro novis blasfematus est, o.
qui pro novis crucifixus est, o.
qui pro novis fele et aceto potatus est, o.
qui pro novis mortuus est, o.
qui pro novis lanceatus est, o.
qui pro novis sepultus est, o.
Domine, miserere quia pecavimus tibi.
Domine, miserere quia pecavimus tibi.
Domine, miserere quia pecavimus tibi.

---

[689] *o*: abbreviation for *ora pro nobis*. The fourteen invocations are in cursive script of the fifteenth century. They cover the entire page and are nearly illegible.

BIBLIOGRAPHY

Aldea Vaquero, Quintín, et al. *Diccionario de historia eclesiástica de España.* Madrid: CSIC, 1972.

Alonso Getino, Luis G. "Centenario y Cartulario de nuestra Comunidad." *La Ciencia Tomista* 19 (1919): 5-20, 127-43, 253-72; 20 (1919): 5-21, 129-52, 265-88.

Anderson, Bonnie S., and Judith P. Zinsser. *A History of Their Own; Women in Europe from Prehistory to the Present.* Vol. I. New York: Harper & Row, 1988.

Aquinas, Thomas. "On Faith." *Summa theologiae.* Part 2-2, Questions 1-16. Translated with Introduction and Notes by Mark D. Jordan. London: U of Notre Dame Press, 1990.

Arenal, Electa, and Stacey Schlau. *Untold Sisters: Hispanic Nuns in Their Own Works.* Albuquerque: U of New Mexico P, 1989.

Bede, the Venerable, Saint. *Bedae Venerabilis Opera.* Ed. D. Hurst. Book II, Parts III and IV. Tvrnholti: Typographi Brepols, 1955.

Blume, Clemens, and Guido M. Dreves, eds. *Analecta hymnica medii aevi.* Vol. XLII. Leipzig: Achte Folge, 1903.

Bonniwell, William R. *A History of the Dominican Liturgy.* 2nd ed. New York: J. F. Wagner, 1945.

Bourassé, Joannes Jacobus, ed. *Summa Aurea de Laudibus Beatissimæ Virginis Mariæ.* Vol. I. Paris: J.-P. Migne, 1862.

Breve tratado que se llama arte de bien morir. Madrid, Biblioteca Nacional, MS 6485.

Brown, Michelle P. *A Guide to Western Historical Scripts from Antiquity to*

112

1600. London: The British Library, 1990.

Butler, Alban. *The Lives of the Fathers, Martyrs, and Other Principal Saints.* Vol. II. New York: P. J. Kenedy and Sons, 1895.

Byrnes, Aquinas. *The Hymns of the Dominican Missal and Breviary.* St. Louis: B. Herder Book Co., 1943.

Constanza de Castilla. *Devocio y oficio.* Madrid, Biblioteca Nacional, MS 7495.

Corominas, Joan. *Diccionario crítico etimológico de la lengua castellana.* 4 vols. Berna, 1954; reprint, 1970.

Delaney, John J., and James Edward Tobin, eds. *Dictionary of Catholic Biography.* Garden City, NY: Doubleday, 1961.

Diccionario de autoridades. 3 vols. Madrid: Editorial Gredos, S.A., 1969.

Dictionnaire de spiritualité, ascétique et mystique: Doctrine et histoire. Vol. VII, Part 2. Paris: Beauchesne, 1971.

Domínguez Bordona, Jesús. *Manuscritos con pinturas.* Vol. I. Madrid: Blass, S.A., 1933.

Doyle, Leonard J., ed. *The Hours of the Divine Office in English and Latin.* 3 vols. Collegeville, MN: The Liturgical Press, 1963.

Fischer, Bonifatio et al., eds. *Biblia Sacra Juxta Vulgatam Versionem.* 3rd rev. ed. Vols. I and II. Stuttgart: Deutsche Bibelgesellschaft, 1983.

Foulet, Alfred, and Mary Blakely Speer. *On Editing Old French Texts.* Lawrence: The Regents Press of Kansas, 1979.

Frere, Walter H., ed. *Graduale Sarisburiense.* London: Plainsong and Mediaeval Music Society, 1894; reprint 1966.

The Greek and Latin Creeds, with Translations. 1877. New York: Harper & Row, 1919. Vol. II of *The Creeds of Christendom with A History and Critical Notes by Philip Schaff.* 3 vols.

Guidelines for Scholarly Editions. New York: Committee on Scholarly Editions, MLA, 1990.

Harper, John. *The Forms and Orders of Western Liturgy.* Oxford: Clarendon Press, 1991.

Historia del Rey Don Pedro, y su descendencia, que es el linage de los Castillas. Escrita por Gracia Dei, glosado y anotado por otro autor, quien va continuando la dicha descendencia. Ed. Antonio Valladares de Sotomayor. In *Semanario Erudito* 28 (1790): 222-88; 29 (1790): 3-61.

Hoyos, Manuel María de los. *Registro documental material inédito dominicano español.* Valladolid: Editorial Sever-Cuesta, 1963.

— *Registro historial de la Provincia de España.* Part 2, Vol. III. Villalva-Pamplona: Editorial OPE, 1968.

Huélamo San José, Ana María. "El devocionario de la dominica Sor

113

Constanza." *Boletín de la Asociación Española de Archiveros, Bibliotecarios, Museólogos y Documentalistas* 42:2 (1992): 133-47.

Hughes, Andrew. *Medieval Manuscripts for Mass and Office: A Guide to Their Organization and Terminology.* Toronto: U of Toronto P, 1982.

Inventario General de Manuscritos de la Biblioteca Nacional. Vol. XII. Madrid: Ministerio de Cultura, 1988.

Jacobus de Voragine. *The Golden Legend.* Trans. William Granger Ryan. 2 vols. Princeton, NJ: Princeton UP, 1993.

Janini, José, and José Serano. *Manuscritos litúrgicos de la Biblioteca Nacional.* Madrid: Dirección General de Archivos y Bibliotecas, 1969.

Johnson, Penelope D. *Equal in Monastic Profession; Religious Women in Medieval France.* Chicago: U of Chicago P, 1991.

Kleinhenz, Christopher, ed. *Medieval Manuscripts and Textual Criticism.* North Carolina Studies in the Romance Languages and Literatures; no. 4. Chapel Hill: U of North Carolina, 1976.

Leroquais, V. *Les Livres d'Heures manuscrits de la Bibliothèque Nationale.* 3 vols. Paris, 1927.

Libro devocionario y horas. Madrid, Biblioteca Nacional, MS 6539.

Lightfoot, J. B. *The Apostolic Fathers.* Part 2. London: Macmillan, 1885.

López, Fray Juan. *Tercera parte de la historia general de Sancto Domingo y de su orden de predicadores.* Valladolid, 1613.

MacBain, William. *De Sainte Katerine; An Anonymous Picard Version of the Life of St. Catherine of Alexandria.* Fairfax, VA: George Mason UP, 1987.

Martène, Edmond. *De Antiquis Ecclesiae Ritibus Libri.* Vol. I. Antwerp, 1736; reprint Hildesheim: George Olms, 1967.

Menéndez Pidal, Ramón. *Manual de gramática histórica española.* 12th ed. Madrid: Espasa-Calpe, S. A., 1966.

Morreale, Margherita. "Los *Gozos* de la Virgen en el *Libro* de Juan Ruiz (II)." *Revista de Filología Española* 64 (1984): 1-69.

New Catholic Encyclopedia. New York: McGraw-Hill, 1989.

O'Connor, Sister Mary Catharine. *The Art of Dying Well: The Development of the "Ars moriendi."* New York: Columbia UP, 1942.

Oliveri, Mauritii Benedicti, ed. *Breviarium Juxta Ritum Sacri Ordinis Praedicatorum.* Parts 1 and 2. Rome, 1834.

Pfaff, R. W. *New Liturgical Feasts in Later Medieval England.* Oxford: Clarendon Press, 1970.

Rubin, Miri. *Corpus Christi. The Eucharist in Late Medieval Culture.* Cambridge: Cambridge UP, 1991.

Sánchez Mariana, Manuel. *Introducción al libro manuscrito*. Madrid: Arco Libros, 1995.

Sheppard, Lancelot C. *The Mass in the West*. Book 114 in Faith and Fact Books; Catholic Truth in the Scientific Age. X. The Worship of the Church. Gen. ed. Lancelot C. Sheppard. London: Burns & Oates, 1962.

Sidwell, Keith. *Reading Medieval Latin*. Cambridge: Cambridge UP, 1995.

Sinclair, Keith V. *French Devotional Texts of the Middle Ages: A Bibliographic Manuscript Guide*. Westport, CN: Greenwood, 1979.

Soleil, Félix. *Les Heures gothiques et la littérature pieuse aux XVe et XVIe siècles*. Rouen: Augé, 1882.

Speer, Mary B. "Editing Old French Texts in the Eighties: Theory and Practice." *Romance Philology* 14.1 (Aug. 1991): 7-43.

Surtz, Ronald E. *Writing Women in Late Medieval and Early Modern Spain*. Philadelphia: U of Pennsylvania P, 1995.

Thurston, Herbert. *Familiar Prayers. Their Origin and History*. Westminster, MD: The Newman P, 1953.

Warner, Marina. *Alone of All Her Sex: The Myth and Cult of the Virgin Mary*. New York: Knopf, 1976.

115

INDEX OF LINGUISTIC CITATIONS

INDEX OF SCRIPTURAL CITATIONS

TABLE OF CONTENTS

ADN-7293

8/4/98
App

BX
2179
C65
B6
1998